Giving Academic Presentations

D1318566

Giving Academic Presentations

Susan M. Reinhart

MICHIGAN SERIES IN ENGLISH FOR
ACADEMIC & PROFESSIONAL PURPOSES

Series Editors John M. Swales and Carolyn G. Madden

Ann Arbor

THE UNIVERSITY OF MICHIGAN PRESS

To my nieces and nephew

Alex
Liz
Adrienne
Robin
Caroline
Kim
Ted

With love

Acknowledgments

I am fortunate to have two colleagues at the English Language Institute, University of Michigan, without whose assistance the text would not have been written. Christine Feak helped me envision the text, contributed materials to three of the units, and evaluated portions of the text; John Swales, former director of the ELI, reviewed the text and provided extensive comments. I also owe a debt of gratitude to Scott Baxter and his students at the School of English, Adam Mickiewicz University, Poznań, Poland, who classroom tested the manuscript and provided valuable feedback. Thanks to Rita Simpson, MICASE Project Manager, for her invaluable training in the use of MICASE and for providing me with scripts and corpus studies. Thanks, also, to those speakers who allowed me to use their speech excerpts and to Sarah Briggs and the helpful MICASE office staff.

Judy Dyer offered feedback on materials she used in her class. Pamela Bogart provided task 5 in unit 3. Philomena Meechan at the Language Resource Center gave me technical advice. Carolyn Madden supported me during the publishing process, and Roann Altman and Meg Rosse gave useful suggestions for improving the manuscript. Many other colleagues answered questions, shared ideas, offered food. Anonymous reviewers gave me many suggestions on how to improve the text.

Thanks to my father, Fred Reinhart, for always offering me a welcoming, quiet place to visit, and to Margo Czinski and Ann Sinsheimer for their friendship, encouragement, and support.

Different versions of this text were classroom tested for over three years in my Academic Speaking class at the English Language Institute. I am deeply indebted to all my students who graciously participated with me in the textbook writing process. Their contributions are found throughout the text.

Contents

Introduction

Many university-enrolled students find themselves unprepared for the task of giving oral presentations on academic material in their area of studies. *Giving Academic Presentations* is an academic speaking text specifically written to prepare university-level students to make presentations in an academic setting. To carry out this goal, the text addresses a range of skills and strategies that speakers of academic English need to become successful presenters. It provides information and hands-on tasks designed to enhance a speaker's performance and thereby maximize communication with members of the audience—faculty, fellow students, and colleagues.

Giving Academic Presentations was primarily written for advanced nonnative speakers of English who are attending or will attend a university-level academic program in English and who are expected, as part of their studies, to make academic presentations. The text has been classroom tested primarily with graduate students but has also been used successfully with undergraduates. The materials were designed for presenters from a range of academic fields; discipline-specific material has been excluded. Instructors who work with international students planning to become teaching assistants (TAs) or graduate student instructors (GSIs) may also wish to consider using this book. While the text does not address teacher-student classroom interaction, it does focus on a number of skills needed for good teaching. The text has been used and perhaps would best be used with students who are not yet ready for advanced TA or GSI English courses. For suggestions for using the text with pre-TAs/GSIs see the Notes to the Instructor that are available on the Web.

Giving Academic Presentations can also be successfully used with native speakers. However, since it was written with nonnative speakers in mind, instructors of native speakers should be cautious when using the text. They may have to add, eliminate, or adapt materials through a process of trial and error. Suggestions for using the text with native speakers are provided in the Notes to the Instructor.

This book teaches skills as diverse as choosing an appropriate topic, creating effective visuals, using the blackboard, and designing a speech opening. While some aspects of speech giving are emphasized, such as awareness and use of common speech types and organizational strategies, one important aim of the text is to make presenters aware that giving an effective presentation requires mastery of a broad range of skills.

The diversity of skills included in *Giving Academic Presentations* is reflected in the following summary of its contents.

- Analysis of speeches to help speakers become more aware of the thought process involved in speech planning

- Examination of major speech types and accompanying organizational strategies

- Work with linking words or signposts and discussion of how they can be successfully used with different types of speeches to enhance the speech flow

- Examination of introductions to speeches, including designing openers and choosing and organizing introductory material

- Discussion of the importance of overviews or summary outlines of speeches; suggestions for designing overviews and visuals to accompany them

- Ways to improve nonverbal behavior

- Suggestions for speaker-listener interaction including

    checking for understanding
    requesting questions from the audience
    preparing and responding to questions from the audience
    interrupting the speaker to ask questions or ask for clarification

- Discussion of the importance of using evidence in academic speaking and the advantage of using certain types of evidence

- Examination of ways to qualify claims and strategies for making weaker or stronger claims

- Definition and discussion of fillers

- Advice on preparing, improving, and using visual aids and making transparencies

- Presentation of practical information about when and how to use an overhead projector and blackboard as well as a discussion of LCD players

- Pronunciation work on pausing, stress, and intonation

- Practical advice about preparing and practicing speeches

- Opportunities for presenters to evaluate their own and others' work

The text is organized into six units; the first five highlight different types of speeches. A typical unit begins with a brief introduction that explains the rationale for choosing the speech type and its relevance to users of the text. The introduction is followed by a speech to be analyzed and questions to guide the discussion. Answers to the questions are then briefly summarized. The rest of the unit concentrates on specific speech-making skills. Suggestions for preparing the presentation are also offered. The final task is the presentation itself. Evaluation sheets and checklists are included in each unit. Each unit contains a "Supplementary Materials" section that includes additional teaching materials and, in all units but the last, a pronunciation section.

The Michigan Corpus of Academic Spoken English (MICASE)

Sections of the text, especially those related to improving speaker-listener interaction, incorporate examples from the University of Michigan English Language Institute's collection of academic spoken English, the Michigan Corpus of Academic Spoken English (MICASE). (R. C. Simpson, S. L. Briggs, J. Ovens, and J. M. Swales, compilers. 1999–2000. The Michigan Corpus of Academic Spoken English. Ann Arbor, MI. The Regents of the University of Michigan. Reproduced with permission of MICASE.) MICASE contains speech events in various academic settings, including lectures, student and faculty panels, and one-on-one discussions. The first of its kind in the United States, this corpus is extremely useful for textbook writers because it contains language that speakers of academic English have actually spoken. Information about MICASE and currently available transcripts are on the Web: <www.hti.umich.edu/m/micase/>.

Notes to the Instructor

A teacher's manual, Notes to the Instructor, is available on the Web for use with this text. It gives both general advice on how to use the text and specific suggestions for using and supplementing material in each unit. Suggestions for additional instructor-designed activities are also included.

Comments and feedback on the text can be sent to susanrei@umich.edu.

Giving an Introduction Speech

When we think about making academic presentations, we probably don't think about making introductions. However, introductions are a part of many academic situations. For example, when a new colleague joins our department, we may introduce him or her to other colleagues. Similarly, at a national meeting we often informally introduce one colleague to another. There may also be times when we find ourselves making introductions in more formal contexts, such as introducing a guest speaker to an audience at a conference or seminar.

We may also introduce ourselves. For example, we may visit advisers, professors, or mentors to share relevant background information about ourselves. Or, in a more formal setting, we might be expected to provide information about ourselves as proof of our expertise, such as when presenting a conference talk, or interviewing for a research or student graduate instructor (teaching assistant) position.

In this unit you will make a presentation in which you introduce one of your fellow students to the rest of the class. Before preparing an academic speech, it is important to consider

Audience
Purpose
Organization

Sizing Up Your Audience

Your audience will determine the shape of your speech—everything from content to organization to presentation style. For your speeches in this class, your audience will generally consist of your fellow students and your instructor.

1. Size up your audience. What characteristics of the audience members should you take into account when planning and presenting an introduction speech?

2. How is this audience similar to or different from one you would encounter in your own department?

Clarifying Your Purpose

The purpose of an introduction speech may vary. For instance, in a social-academic context you may want to help establish a network among peers. When introducing a speaker at a conference, your purpose may be to establish his or her credibility.

1. Besides providing the opportunity for you to speak in front of the class, what might the purpose of this introduction speech be?

Organizing Your Speech

Organizing a speech is probably the single most important task of a good presenter. If your speech is well organized, the audience will likely be able to follow you, even if your grammar and pronunciation are not totally accurate. As you work through the text, you will become familiar with several major organizational patterns in English. Depending on the type of speech you are making and the information you want to convey, one or more patterns will form the structure of your presentation.

▩ Task 1: Organizing an Introduction Speech

Below are outlines of two introduction speeches. Working in small groups or pairs, answer the following questions.

- How is speech 1 organized?
- Is speech 2 organized the same way? Explain.

Speech 1	Speech 2
Introduction of partner: name and country	Introduction of partner: name and country
B.S. degree (1992)	Educational background
1st job—military (1992)	• B.A. degree
2nd job (1994)	• M.A. degree
M.A. degree + award (1998)	• Current studies
3rd job (1999)	Work experience
	• 1st job
Current studies and research assistantship.	• 2nd job
• major	• current job—research assistant
• research area of interest	
	Extracurricular activities
Current interests	• Skiing
• family: new baby	• Computer games
• American football	
	Closing
Closing	

Both speakers use chronological order (arrangement of information in order of their time of occurrence, here from past to present). The difference is that the first speaker uses only chronological order, while the second also uses classification (organization of information by category). The second speaker first organizes her speech into three major sections: educational background, work experience, and extracurricular activities. Then, where possible, she uses chronological order to arrange information within the categories.

A First Look at Linking Words: Time Connectors

The organizational pattern you choose generally lends itself to the use of specific linking words or signposts. Linking words are words that connect information to create a smooth, coherent flow of speech. Time connectors are frequently used to connect events. In addition, they sometimes function to inform the audience of a topic shift. One example of a topic shift in speech 1 above would be a shift from the person's current studies to his current interests. What could be an example of a topic shift in speech 2?

Task 2

Read the three examples that follow. In each example, the speaker uses time expressions and time connectors to relate events to each other. One of the time connectors in each example is used to indicate a shift from one subtopic to another. With your partner, write down these time connectors in the box provided. Then write the old topic and the new topic.

Example	Topic Shift Time Connector	Old Topic	New Topic
1. Wei worked in a pharmaceutical company for three years. While he was there, he did research on a drug for the treatment of arthritis. In 1998, he went back to school to get a master's degree in pharmacology.			
2. In high school Adrienne participated in a number of extracurricular activities. She was a member of the drama club, and by the time she graduated she had had the lead in three plays. She was also president of the student government for two years. While she was in high school, Adrienne was offered a job in summer theater in her first professional role.			
3. Last year Marc decided to continue his studies in the U.S. He's now enrolled in a Ph.D. program in political science in the university. His area of interest is campaign financing. Before coming to the U.S. to sudy, Marc worked in two different jobs.*			

*Notice that the speaker refers to the present and then shifts to the past. Why?

Time Connectors: *the following, following*

In addition to words like *after, while, then, during,* and *before,* the words *following* and *the following* can function as time connectors in speeches that are organized chronologically. *The following* generally precedes a time period, such as *the following year, month,* or *week.*

Following, on the other hand, generally precedes a specific event, such as *following my job as a lab technician, retirement, the birth of my child, his two-year internship,* or *high school.* Notice that the event can be an experience that takes place over a period of time.

- During my first semester of college, I majored in art. *The following semester,* however, I switched to architecture.
- *Following graduation,* Sonya had three laboratory jobs.

Organization Indicator Statements

In pairs or groups, look at "Sonya's Work Experience" (it is similar to the "Work Experience" section in the speech outline on p. 3). Then answer the discussion questions that follow.

```
Sonya's Work Experience

   1. 1st job — lab technician

   2. 2nd job — lab supervisor

   3. current job — lab instructor
```

Excerpt A

Following graduation, Sonya first worked as a lab technician. . . . Then she was promoted to lab supervisor. . . . And after that, she became a lab instructor.

Excerpt B

Following graduation, Sonya had three laboratory jobs. First, she worked as a lab technician. . . . Then she was promoted to lab supervisor. . . . And after that, she became a lab instructor.

1. How are excerpts A and B similar, different? Which one do you prefer? Why?

2. In excerpt B, the speaker uses an organization indicator statement, *Following graduation, Sonya had three laboratory jobs,* before listing Sonya's lab jobs. What is its purpose?

Both speakers list their partner's jobs in sequence by using the time connectors *first, then,* and *after that.* However, in excerpt B, the speaker uses an organization indicator statement that summarizes how many jobs Sonya has had in total: *Following graduation, Sonya had three laboratory jobs.* Organization indicator statements or discourse indicator statements are used frequently in academic English. They are procedural in that they tell the audience what information they can expect to hear next and give some indication about how it might be organized.

Beginning Your Speech

There are a number of ways to begin your introduction speech. Some openings may be rather formulaic, others more creative. Which of the following options do you think are effective? Why?

1. Today I'm happy to introduce you to _____ , who recently came to the university from the Czech Republic.

2. Good morning. I'd like to introduce you to _____ , who is a nurse from Bangkok, Thailand.

3. Hi everyone. It's my pleasure to introduce you to someone who never expected to be studying art at this university. His name is _____ .

4. I'm pleased to introduce you to a woman who's interested in stones and bones. She's studying physical anthropology here at the university. Her name is _____ .*

Concluding Your Speech

When you conclude your introduction speech, try to end on a positive note. You may rely on formulaic expressions such as

So let's (please) welcome . . .
I'm sure we'll all enjoy getting to know . . .

Avoid an abrupt ending such as *So that's all* or *I'm done.*

▧ Task 3: Gathering Information

Working in pairs, interview your partner. Gather enough information to enable you to develop a three- to four-minute introduction speech. First, concentrate on collecting information about your partner's educational and professional experience and current academic interests. Then take some time to ask your partner about family, extracurricular activities, and other nonacademic interests. If you are interviewing an undergraduate who has had little professional experience, include questions about participation in high school and community organizations, awards, travel, volunteer work, and short-term jobs.

If you wish, list the questions that you plan to ask your partner during the interview in the box that follows. Then write down the notes you collect about your partner.

---

*Notice that at the beginning of this speech, the speaker tells the audience what the woman's current position is. This strategy of first situating the woman in her present context is common and does not preclude the speaker from (1) using chronological order to organize the rest of the speech or (2) elaborating on the woman's current position later in the speech.

Questions	Notes

▧ Task 4: Further Considerations

Read the following introductory excerpt. As you read the excerpt, think about what changes you would make. Use the questions that follow as a guide for group discussion.

> The pretty lady I'm going to introduce you to today is
> Carolina from San José. Carolina lives at 30 Stone Hill
> Lane in case you want to visit her. Carolina is a first-year
> master's student in the School of Nursing. She began to
> show an interest in medicine at the age of four when her
> brother stepped on her cat's tail. She responded quickly
> by bandaging the tail in adhesive tape.

| Discussion Questions |

1. What information has the speaker included in this introductory excerpt that you would omit? Why?

2. What information has the speaker left out that you would include? Why?

3. Why do you think the speaker mentions the cat story? Would you keep the story or eliminate it?

In a more casual or collegial academic setting, introduce a person by both his/her first and last name (e.g., *Carolina Mendoza*) and then refer to the person by his/her first name (*Carolina*). In a more formal academic setting, also begin by saying the person's complete name (e.g., *Mohammad Aziz*). Depending on the situation, it may be appropriate to include the person's title, such as Professor, Doctor, or Dean. You may wish to ask the person how he or she would like to be referred to after your opening. However, if you feel uncomfortable calling the person by his or her first name, simply continue to use the person's title (e.g., *Dr. Aziz*). Men with no specific title can be referred to as *Mr.* and women as *Ms.,* unless they prefer *Miss* or *Mrs.*

Avoid referring to the person you introduce as *lady, girl, gal,* or *guy* even in an informal setting. These references are not considered appropriate. Instead, use *person.*

Focus on the academic and professional information you gathered. To avoid embarrassing your partner, (1) exclude personal information about your partner, such as phone number, age, and address, and (2) avoid reference to your partner's physical attributes, such as how attractive s/he is.

Include background information that the audience might need, such as geographical locations *(San José, Costa Rica,* or *San José, the capital of Costa Rica).*

When using humor, keep your audience and purpose in mind. Audiences respond to humor, if it is used appropriately. By adding humor to your speech, you may heighten audience interest. This in turn may make you feel more relaxed. Sometimes speakers plan to use humor in their presentation; other times it arises spontaneously from the circumstances.

Task 5: Nervousness

Everyone is somewhat nervous when speaking before a group for the first time, but nervousness will diminish as you have more opportunities to make presentations. In the list that follows, check the concerns that you have now. Throughout the course, you will be able to address these concerns with your instructor and other members of the class.

___ 1. I'm worried that other students won't understand me because of my pronunciation.

___ 2. I think I'll forget what I want to say when I stand in front of a group.

___ 3. I feel uncomfortable making eye contact with the audience.

___ 4. I think the other students will be bored because I speak slowly in English.

___ 5. I am afraid that I will not be able to express myself clearly.

Write down one or two other concerns you have and share them with your partner or the class.

___ 6.

___ 7.

Nonverbal Behavior

Because of your concerns or nervousness, you may unknowingly engage in behavior that may detract from your speech. Behavior that can detract from your presentation include

Avoiding eye contact with the audience

- Looking at the ceiling, out the window, at the floor, or at the camera
- Staring at one member of the audience, or at only one section of the room
- Looking at notes to avoid eye contact with the audience

Avoiding friendly facial expressions

- Maintaining a serious, unchanging facial expression

Making distracting body movements

- Pulling on your shirtsleeve
- Pacing back and forth or shuffling your feet

- Taking your hands in and out of your pockets
- Playing with objects in your hand (papers, transparencies, pens, keys, etc.)

Avoiding the use of hand gestures

- Grasping your hands behind your back or in front of you
- Keeping your hands in your pockets or "glued" to your side
- Holding something in your hand, such as a pen, large piece of paper, or pointer

Other distracting behaviors

- Laughing nervously
- Gum chewing or snapping

Tips for Improving Nonverbal Communication

- Hand gestures will be discussed more fully in unit 4. In the meantime, keep your hands empty of unnecessary objects and avoid grasping or hiding your hands. This way your hands will be left free to gesture naturally.

- If you think you may have trouble establishing eye contact with the audience or tend to focus on only one or two listeners, try dividing the audience into three or four groups. Move your eyes from one group to another, making sure to include the groups to your far left and far right. If you feel uncomfortable looking directly at people's eyes, look at another part of their face, such as their nose.

- Try to maintain a friendly, open relationship with your audience. Even if you are nervous, listeners will appreciate your positive attitude and you may actually become more relaxed.

■ Task 6: Approaches to Preparing and Delivering Your Speech

Here are a number of approaches to preparing and delivering your speech. Working with a partner, choose the ones you would use to help you prepare and deliver a speech. Discuss your responses with the class.

___ 1. Checking the accuracy of your information.

___ 2. Writing out your speech word for word.

___ 3. Reading your speech.

___ 4. Memorizing your speech word for word.

___ 5. Preparing notes on a small note card and using the note card if you forget what you were going to say.

___ 6. Practicing your speech once before class, assuming you'll do a good job when you get to class.

___ 7. Practicing your speech silently in your head.

___ 8. Rehearsing and timing your speech five to six times in front of a mirror.

___ 9. Recording your speech either on audio- or videotape before class and evaluating yourself.

The importance of practice

Practice your speech three times orally, standing in front of a mirror. Then record it one or two times and evaluate yourself. Make changes and practice again. Ask a colleague or family member to listen to you and give you feedback. Practice will help you feel better prepared and thus more confident. You will have fewer hesitations and will be able to remember the contents of your speech better, making it possible to speak with no notes or a small note card. Practice will also help you avoid translating from your native language.

When you practice, keep in mind that minor grammar errors generally don't interfere with the audience's ability to understand you. Also, if you forget to include a few details, the audience probably won't be aware of these omissions.

▓ Task 7: Presentation

Prepare a short three- to four-minute formal introduction of your partner. First, interview your partner. Then decide what information you would like to include in your speech. Be sure to find out how you can contact your partner, in case you need additional information.

1. Carefully organize your speech, using one or more of the organizing strategies you've learned.

2. Use linking words so that the audience can follow you. When organizing, use time connectors, especially during topic shifts. Use an organizational indicator statement before listing several events in sequence.

3. Plan a short introduction and conclusion. In your introduction, you may first wish to tell the audience your partner's current academic or professional position and then discuss the events that led up to it.

4. If you think you will forget your speech, make a small note card about the size of the box below with your outline on it. A large piece of paper may distract attention from the audience. Don't read your speech or memorize it word for word. Instead, refer to the note card to help you remember what you are going to say.

5. Practice your speech out loud and standing two to three times. Pay attention to nonverbal behavior that may detract from or enhance your speech. Then record your speech using an audio- or videotape. Listen to your presentation and decide what sections need improvement. Use the Introduction Speech Evaluation Form as a guide. Then practice it several more times. Ask a colleague or family member to listen to your speech and give you feedback as well.

Introduction Speech Outline

(Put your outline on a note card about this size).

Prespeech Evaluation

After practicing your speech three to four times, record it and then fill in the following self-evaluation form.

Introduction Speech Evaluation Form			
Name: _____			

	(Make a check in the appropriate column)			
	Good	OK	Needs Work	Comments (include specific problems you noticed)
Topic information Interesting? Suitable for this audience?				
Introduction Adequate? Attention-getting?				
Organization Clear organizational strategy? Used organization indicator statement(s) when appropriate?				
Linking words (signposts) Smooth, coherent speech flow? Correct use of time expressions and other connectors?				
Conclusion Adequate? Smooth, not abrupt?				
Eye contact and facial expressions Focus on the audience? Contact with all members of the audience? Friendly facial expression?				
Gestures and other body movements Hands free and expressive? Body posture relaxed rather than stiff? No distracting body movements?				

| | (Make a check in the appropriate column) | | | |
	Good	OK	Needs Work	Comments (include specific problems you noticed)
Voice Good volume? Confident? Relaxed?				
Pace Not too fast or too slow? Smooth rather than halting or hesitant?				
Pronunciation (specific problems)				
Other comments				
Goals for my next presentation (list 2–3 areas that you want to improve on for your next presentation)				

Final Evaluation

Listen to your final speech. Then, fill in the final Introduction Speech Evaluation Form below. Be sure to provide specific comments in the "Other comments" section. Also, set goals for your next speech.

If you would like to evaluate your speech with one or two partners, together discuss your strengths and weaknesses and then fill in the evaluation form. If you wish, include feedback from your partners on the form.

A sample completed evaluation is provided.

Introduction Speech Evaluation Form

Name: _____

	(Make a check in the appropriate column)			
	Good	OK	Needs Work	Comments (include specific problems you noticed)
Topic information Interesting? Suitable for this audience?				
Introduction Adequate? Attention-getting?				
Organization Clear organizational strategy? Used organization indicator statement(s) when appropriate?				
Linking words (signposts) Smooth, coherent speech flow? Correct use of time expressions and other connectors?				
Conclusion Adequate? Smooth, not abrupt?				
Eye contact and facial expressions Focus on the audience? Contact with all members of the audience? Friendly facial expression?				

	(Make a check in the appropriate column)			
	Good	OK	Needs Work	Comments (include specific problems you noticed)
Gestures and other body movements Hands free and expressive? Body posture relaxed rather than stiff? No distracting body movements?				
Voice Good volume? Confident? Relaxed?				
Pace Not too fast or too slow? Smooth rather than halting or hesitant?				

Pronunciation

(specific problems)

Other comments

Goals for my next presentation (list 2–3 areas that you want to improve on for your next presentation)

Sample Completed Evaluation

Introduction Speech Evaluation Form

Name: _____

	(Make a check in the appropriate column)			
	Good	OK	Needs Work	Comments (include specific problems you noticed)
Topic information Interesting? Suitable for this audience?		✓		It was pretty good but my partner suggested that I give more details about Juan's work experience. (Good idea.)
Introduction Adequate? Attention-getting?	✓			Good. I used a little humor.
Organization Clear organizational strategy? Used organization indicator statement(s) when appropriate?	✓			I organized by chronological order and used an organization indicator statement "Juan has had two research positions at the university."
Linking words (signposts) Smooth, coherent speech flow? Correct use of time expressions and other connectors?	✓			I think I successfully used time connectors.
Conclusion Adequate? Smooth, not abrupt?		✓		Good, but at the end I said, "I'm finished." It wasn't necessary.
Eye contact and facial expressions Focus on the audience? Contact with all members of the audience? Friendly facial expression?			✓	I hardly looked at the audience because I was nervous. I looked at my notes even though I didn't need them.
Gestures and other body movements Hands free and expressive? Body posture relaxed rather than stiff? No distracting body movements?		✓		I moved my right hand but kept my left hand in my pocket.

	(Make a check in the appropriate column)			
	Good	OK	Needs Work	Comments (include specific problems you noticed)
Voice Good volume? Confident? Relaxed?			✓	My voice was too soft. Both partners said it was a little hard to hear me.
Pace Not too fast or too slow? Smooth rather than halting or hesitant?	✓			I practiced a lot so I didn't have a lot of pauses.

Pronunciation
(specific problems)   two thousand (2000) — I said two tousand

Other comments

I wore my coat during my speech. It wasn't necessary.

Goals for my next presentation (list 2–3 areas that you want to improve on for your next presentation)

1. Include more details to keep the audience's attention
2. Use more eye contact
3. Speak louder

Unit 1 Supplementary Materials

Pronunciation: Pausing

During their speeches, some presenters speak too slowly and haltingly, while others speak too quickly. Both of these problems can be helped with proper pausing.

Speaking too slowly.

When presenters pause too much, they seem unprepared because their presentations are choppy or hesitant. This may be because they pause after every word or two and also repeat words or parts of words too often. If you think you pause too much, one helpful suggestion is to practice more. When practicing, try to say a group of several words before pausing. That way, the speech flow will seem smoother to the listener. The more confident you become, the less you will pause and the longer your groupings will be. Examples of natural groupings in English are

Example	Grouping
Right now,*	linking word (adverb)
John's studying business	subject + verb + object
at the University of Michigan	prepositional phrase
His major area of interest	noun phrase
[is] managing nonprofit corporations	noun phrase
Before John went to college,	subordinate clause
he traveled around the world for two years.	main clause

What is pausing? In this section, pauses are defined in two ways.

1. **When the speaker makes a complete stop.** Speakers may come to a complete stop at the end of a sentence, for example to take a breath or to begin a topic shift (see p. 4), as in

   > John's major area of interest is managing nonprofit corporations. *(Pause stop)* Before John went to college, he traveled around the world for two years.

---

*Speakers may find it useful to pause after adverbs that function as linking words, such as *currently, consequently, however,* and *nevertheless,* that occur at the beginning of a sentence.

2. **When the speaker rests, slows down, or lingers at a particular point, such as at the end of the word grouping.** Because the speaker slows down but does not stop, s/he links the word before the pause to the word after the pause. In this example,

> John's major area of interest is managing nonprofit corporations. Before John went to college *(pause slow down),* he traveled around the world for two years.

> In this example, the speaker slows down at *college* and then links it to the next word, *he.* The word *college* is slightly extended or lengthened and then flows into *he (collegeĥe).**

Say the passage that follows, slowing down after the groupings marked with //. Link the word before the pause to the word that follows. Make a complete stop after groupings marked with ////. Try to minimize rather than eliminate other pauses.

> Right now, // John's studying business // at the University of Michigan. ////
>
> His major area of interest // is managing nonprofit corporations. //// Before
>
> John went to college, // he traveled around the world for two years. ////

Speaking too quickly

Presenters who speak too quickly have a tendency to forget to pause at the end of natural word groupings in English. This puts extra demands on listeners who need time to absorb information. Speakers who speak too fast can modify their speed simply by adding pauses in such places as after linking words (e.g., *right now*) and prepositional phrases (e.g., *during the last two summers*) that occur at the beginning of a sentence, and at the ends of sentences, especially when making a topic shift.

▨ Task 8: Excerpt from an Introduction Speech

Practice saying the following speech using the pause markers to guide you. Symbols for the types of pauses mentioned above are // for slow down, //// for stop. If you find yourself pausing after every word or two, add several more pause markers to make shorter word groupings and attempt to pause only where you have placed pause markers. If you are speaking too quickly, use a reminder such as saying *pause* to yourself before continuing, especially at the end of each sentence.

---

*The *h* sound is generally dropped in American English because *he* is unstressed.

Claire got a B.A. in natural resources in 1997. //// During college, // she did research on fish decline in the Great Lakes. //// After graduation, // she interned at a research institute // that studies environmental changes in the Great Lakes. //// Three years later, // she returned to the university to get a master's degree in natural resources. ////

Task 9

After finishing your introduction speech, transcribe four or five sentences from your video- or audiotaped speech. Indicate where you paused and also where you repeated words or parts of words. Do you think that you paused too little or too much? If you think you paused too much, practice grouping words together and pausing after each grouping. Try to minimize rather than eliminate other pauses and word repetition. If you think you spoke too quickly, add pauses after longer word groupings and say the sentences again. If you still find yourself speaking too quickly, try taking a breath or saying *pause* to yourself at natural breaks before continuing. Come to a full stop especially when making a topic shift. Tape yourself again and compare the two performances.

Introducing Colleagues at Conferences and Seminars

At academic conferences and seminars, a guest speaker may be introduced to the audience by one of the organizers or moderators of the event. In this situation, the guest speaker, James Hilton, is being introduced by the director of the Language Resource Center at the University of Michigan, Monika Dressler, at a conference called "Integrating Teaching, Information, and Technology." It was designed for faculty members at the university.

Read the introduction and then answer the following questions. Sentence numbers have been added for your convenience.

Introduction

(1) The title of this opening event is "Two Sides of the Technology Coin: Perspectives on Enhancing Student Learning and Supporting Faculty Scholarship." (2) Our first speaker will present on the first side of the coin—that of enhancing student learning. (3) James Hilton is an Arthur F. Thurnau Professor* and the undergraduate chair in psychology at the University of Michigan. (4) He received his undergraduate degree in psychology from the University of Texas in 1981 and his Ph.D. from the social psychology program at Princeton University in 1985. (5) Among the courses he teaches are Introductory Psychology, Introductory Social Psychology, and Experimental Methods. (6) These courses range in size from 25 to 1,200 students. (7) He is a three-time recipient of the LS&A Excellence in Education Award at the University of Michigan, and (although he doesn't look all that old) he is also the recipient of the Class of 1923 Memorial Teaching Award. (8) His research focuses on expectancy effects, stereotypes, and the psychology of suspicion. (9) Along with Charles Perdue, he is the author of a multimedia CD-ROM in psychology entitled *Longman Mind Matters* published by Addison Wesley Longman. (10) Whew . . . that's his official introduction. (11) To add to this are some adjectives that some of my staff and student workers volunteered: *dynamic, entertaining, dedicated, multifaceted, innovative, funny,* and *really smart.* (12) It is my immense pleasure to welcome our first speaker, James Hilton.

(Introduction by Monika Dressler, with slight modifications, used with permission.)

Discussion Questions

1. What information is included in this introduction?

2. How is the introduction organized?

3. Different purposes and audiences may determine the content and organizational strategy of an introduction speech. Explain how this introduction takes into account the purpose and the audience.

---

*American university professors are distinguished by being given a position that has the name of a former outstanding scholar or contributor.

Notice that the speaker depends less on chronological order than on classification to organize information. Categories she highlights are current teaching responsibilities and awards, research and publications, and praise from colleagues and students. The speaker relies heavily on listing to organize information within categories.

▨ Task 10: Introducing a Speaker at a Conference

Imagine that you have been asked to introduce a speaker at a conference. Introduce your partner or someone that your instructor assigns to you. Like the speaker above, focus on the presenter's more current accomplishments, responsibilities, and interests. You may wish to include

- Degrees
- Recent work history and current work
- Current research interests
- Publications
- Awards
- Praise from others about the speaker

Before concluding your introduction, be sure to include the title of the speaker's presentation.

— Unit 2 —

Describing an Object

In a university setting, both students and faculty describe, explain, and define academic material. For example, we may describe an object, explain a procedure or process, or define a concept. The meanings of the words *describe, explain,* and *define* greatly overlap, and all express the same general intention of the speaker to impart or provide specific information on a given topic. Both the speaker and audience initially work from the assumption that the information is true and generally accurate, or at least what is currently known, unless the speaker indicates otherwise.

The overall goal of units 2, 3, and 4 is to assist you in developing skills for presenting information from your area of studies to a general academic audience. The topics of these units are as follows:

Unit 2: Describing an object

Unit 3: Explaining a process or procedure

Unit 4: Defining a concept

Describing an object in an academic setting is a familiar task. As a part of class or laboratory discussion, instructors and students frequently describe the characteristics and function of important objects in their field of studies. Academics who work with patients in areas such as dentistry, nursing, medicine, and speech pathology describe and explain certain objects as part of their routine. Advanced students may also be called on to discuss objects during a presentation or research project discussion.

What does the term *object* mean? In this unit, *object* is used broadly and is perhaps best explained by providing examples in somewhat informally arranged categories. For instance, objects may be animate, such as a butterfly or a tree, or inanimate, such as a microscope or suspension bridge. Objects may be a part of a larger object or system, such as a computer keyboard or an eye. Many objects, such as a parasite or an atom, cannot be seen by the unaided eye. Some objects are well known to the listener, such as an antenna, while other objects, such as an oscilloscope or a machining center, may be unknown to most listeners. Certain objects, like a pagoda or a totem pole, are familiar to listeners from one part of the world but unfamiliar to listeners from another part. Some objects may consist mainly of a written text with standard parts such as a receipt, a lease, a job application letter, a lab report, a case study, a government document, or a drug insert.

In certain academic areas, such as architecture, engineering, astronomy, computer sciences, biological and medical sciences, geology, and dentistry, describing concrete objects or instruments is far more common than in other academic areas, such as economics, languages and linguistics, women's studies, and public policy, which focus on more abstract concepts. Even though in the future you may have few opportunities to describe an object in your area of studies, this introductory academic speech will help prepare you to

1. Work within the confines of the speech type

2. Choose an appropriate topic for a general academic audience

3. Decide what information to include in your presentation based on factors such as audience and time limits

4. Choose an organizational strategy and linking words that best suit your object

5. Correctly use language that explains the function or purpose of the object and its specific parts

6. Make a visual aid to accompany your speech

In the space that follows, write down several objects from your field of studies. As you go through the tasks in the unit, evaluate these objects as possible topics for your final presentation.

■ Task 1: "Receipt" Speech

This unit begins with a presentation by an international student in economics in which he describes an object. While economics generally deals with more abstract concepts and principles, the topic of this speech is an object that everyone is familiar with.

With a partner or in a small group, read aloud the speech entitled "Receipt." Then answer the questions that follow.

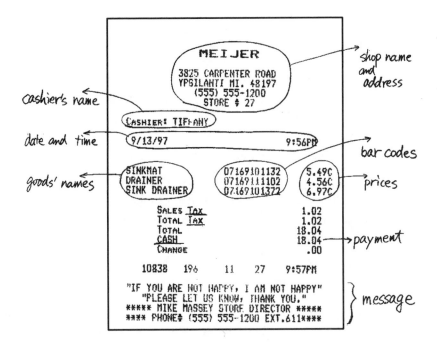

Receipt

1. Hello, everybody.

2. Today I'm talking about an object related with my major. My major is economics, and almost every economic transaction is ended by getting or giving receipts. So I'll talk about what kind of information we can see on a receipt. Let me talk about it from top to the bottom of the receipt.

3. I think you may get receipts every day, but I suppose you don't look at the details of this, so I think it's valuable to explain what kind of information is on the receipt.

4. *(Points to the transparency on the screen)* First, as you can see, this is the name of the shop, store, you know, Meijer. It's a very famous shopping store in town. And this part has very basic information—name and address and phone number so you can see where you get, you bought those goods, from what store.

5. *(Points)* And next, the cashier's name is written here. It's important because for for the store they can know who is responsible for this transaction. Okay?

6. *(Points)* And next is the date and time. These are important for both store and shopper.

7. *(Points)* Below this, these are the items I bought the other day—three items. This is the name of goods—in this case, sink mat. *(Points to "sinkmat")*

8. *(Points)* And this is the bar code. Each good has its unique bar code. This is not important for buyer, but this is very important for seller because they manage, ah, they control what goods are sold or what goods remain in the store by checking these codes.

9. *(Points)* And this is the price, the most concerned part. And below that there is the total price and tax. And this, how I paid. In this case, I paid by cash. If I pay by a credit credit card, I think this is "Charge." So this is the information of the payment.

10. *(Points to the numbers under the word* "Change"*)* And I don't know this part, what it stands for.

11. *(Points)* And the final part is a message from supermarket to customers. Customers don't need this information, uh, so often, but I think this is important for the seller because in this case this message says how much they are concerned with their reputation or customers, how much they care about their customers. *(Points to and reads writing)* In this case, "If you are not happy, I am not happy. Please let us know. Thank you." So if there's any complaint on this store, please let us know. If the customers see this, they think the shop, the store, cares about us.

12. I think is this is a good example for explaining what a receipt is. Thank you.

(Speech by Shuichi Matsuta, with minor modifications.)

Discussion Questions

1. What is the topic and purpose of the speech? Is the topic appropriate for a general academic audience?

2. How does the speaker introduce his topic?

3. What organization strategy does he use? How do you know?

4. Underline some connecting words or signposts the speaker uses to move from one part of the receipt to another. How does the speaker indicate that he has reached the last section of the receipt?

5. What words does the speaker define in his speech?

6. The speaker doesn't actually give a formal definition of the word *receipt.* Why not?

7. Do you think the speaker's visual is effective? Why or why not?

8. What suggestion would you give the speaker for improving his speech?

The speaker begins his speech by putting the topic into an academic context—economics. Then he introduces his topic (receipt) and tells the audience how he has organized the speech: he will talk about the parts from top to bottom. He proceeds to discuss the receipt systematically, going from top to bottom. This strategy makes it easy for him to remember what he is going to say next and for his audience to follow him. He uses signposts such as *first, and this is, below this, and next,* and *and the final part is* to indicate that he is moving on to another part of the receipt.

In this speech, the speaker does not begin with a formal definition of the word *receipt.* He likely assumes that the audience is familiar with the word. However, as the speaker discusses the parts of the receipt, he does attempt to define several terms, such as *Meijer* and *bar code.* So, in designing his speech, he keeps in mind what information the audience needs to follow him.

The speaker chooses a simple visual for his speech, an actual receipt. While it is not flashy or colorful, it is a clear representation of an object that everyone in the audience is familiar with but which they may have paid little attention to.

This receipt represents one of millions of small economic transactions that together have an impact on our society. At the end of his speech, if the speaker had more time, he could lengthen his conclusion slightly to reiterate the importance of receipts.

Organization

In the "Receipt" speech, the speaker organized his speech spatially from top to bottom. In English, four common ways to organize a presentation on an object are

1. From general to specific

2. Spatially

3. From the most important part to the least important part, or vice versa

4. Logically

Keep in mind that in English, speakers may combine several organizational strategies.

1. From general to specific

An object may consist of several major parts. The speaker first introduces the object and then introduces each of its major parts. After that, the speaker returns to each part and describes it in detail, including its subparts. This is an example of general to specific organization.

2. Spatially

An object may have a form or function that lends itself to a specific spatial organizational strategy. There are a variety of ways to organize spatially. They include

- Top to bottom (preferred),* or bottom to top

- Left to right (preferred),* or right to left

- Front to back

- Outside to inside, or inside to outside

- Clockwise or counterclockwise

3. From the most important part to the least important part, or vice versa

The speaker may wish to begin with the most important parts of the object and
then discuss other relevant but less important parts. Or the speaker may begin
with the less important parts and move toward the more important ones.

4. Logically

In order to explain one part of an object to the audience, the speaker may need to
explain another part first. The relationship between the parts of the object can
best be shown using this strategy.

---

*Speakers may prefer these because English is read from left to right, top to bottom. However, the
object itself may reveal the best spatial strategy.

▥ Task 2

In groups, look at the following objects. If you were giving a speech describing one of these objects, which organizational strategy (strategies) would you choose? Why? Where would you begin? How would you proceed?

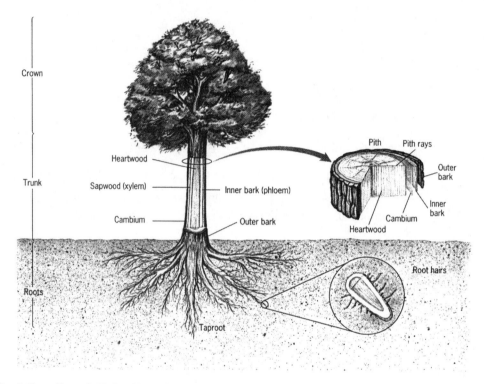

Fig. 1. Tree. (From C. H. Stoddard, _Essentials of Forestry Practice,_ 3d ed. [New York: John Wiley and Sons, 1978]. Copyright © 1978. Reprinted by permission of John Wiley and Sons, Inc.)

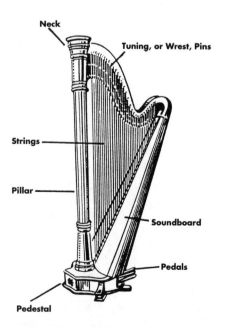

Fig. 2. Harp. (From _The World Book Encyclopedia._ © World Book, Inc. By permission of the publisher. www.worldbook.com.)

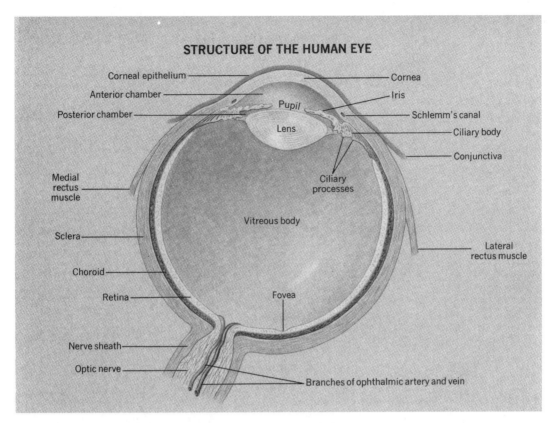

STRUCTURE OF THE HUMAN EYE

Fig. 3. Eye. (From the _Encyclopedia Americana,_ 2001 Edition. Copyright 2001 by Grolier Incorporated. Reprinted with permission from the publisher.)

▨ Task 3

What do you think of this student's proposed organizational strategy for describing the harp? What strategy does he use? Is it similar to or different from your group's strategy? Keep in mind that there may be several ways to organize the information.

The Harp

1. First, I'd introduce and define the harp so that people would know what kind of musical instrument it is: "A harp is a stringed instrument with a large triangular frame made of wood." Here I'll add more background information, for example, that it's the oldest stringed instrument, etc.

2. Then I would move to the parts. I'd begin with the _pedestal, pillar,_ and _neck,_ since they are the column that provides the main support for the instrument.

3. After that, I would introduce the _strings,_ since they create the unique sound of the instrument. I would mention the number of strings and the type of sound they make.

4. Next, I'd talk about the *pins.* I can't mention the pins until I've talked about the strings because the pins are used to tune the strings.

5. Last, I'd discuss the *soundboard* and *pedals,* since they enhance the sound of the strings and provide additional frame support.

Pointing with Words

In English, there are a number of ways to point to, introduce, or name an object. The parts of an object can also be introduced using the same or similar strategies.

- One of the most common ways of introducing an object is by using *this is.*

    This is **a harp.**

    Notice that the article *a* is used when the object is first introduced. The parts of the object can also be introduced by using *This is* (or *These are*). However, the article *the* is generally used instead of *a.*

    These are **the strings.**

- Another common way to point to the parts of an object in English is by using the expression *Here you have.* It has the same function as *this is.*

    Here you have **the pins, which are used to tune the strings.**

- The expression *That is (That's)* is also commonly used, especially when the speaker wishes to spatially relate one part of an object to another.

    This is **the pupil (of the eye), and** ***that's*** **the lens (right behind the pupil).***

    This is can be accompanied by *here* and *that is* by *there.*

    This is **the cornea** ***here*** **and** ***that's*** **the retina** ***there.***

- Speakers can also name a part by using the expression *is (are) called.*

    And this (that) ***is called*** **the bar code.**

---

*Notice that *and* is used in this example and in the next three examples to help move the discussion from one part of the object to another.

- Spatial connectors such as *next* and *after that* and prepositions of location such as *behind, underneath, in back of, next to, inside of* are also used to introduce parts and relate them to each other.*

  And next is the date and time.

  This is the outer bark of the tree, and *behind* **it |is | the inner bark.****

  |you can see|

  |you have |

Nonverbal Behavior: Pointing with Your Hands

Some speakers like to use a pointing device when introducing the parts of an object. Pointing devices may not be necessary and can even be distracting. Novice speakers should instead use their hand to point. Pointing finds a use for the speaker's hand and helps the speaker look more natural.

One frequently asked question is, "Where should the speaker stand when using an overhead projector?" A speaker who stands next to an overhead projector (OHP) will find it difficult to gesture and in addition may be tempted to look down at the transparency on the OHP instead of at the audience. On the other hand, if the speaker stands to the left or right of the screen, he or she can gesture more easily at the object on the screen and will be in a better position to make eye contact with members of the audience.

Describing an Object

There are a number of ways to describe an object or its parts. One common way is to describe its shape *(triangular, square, round, heart-shaped, curved, wavy, oblong, spiral)*. Another is to mention the material it is made of *(wood, metal, plastic, rubber, glass)*. A third way is to use adjectives that describe its characteristics, such as *flexible, pliable, coarse, rough, smooth, thin, heavy, woven, fragile,*

---

*In the "Receipt" speech, the speaker used *next* as a spatial connector, as in *next is the date and time.* It is interesting to note that *then* cannot be used as a spatial connector with *be* but can be used with *you have* or *you can see* (*then you have, then you can see,* but not *then is*).

**In English we frequently highlight new information by putting it at the end of the sentence. In this case, the new information is the next part of the object to be introduced. Therefore, it is less likely that we would say, *This is the outer bark of the tree, and the inner bark is behind it.*

delicate, shiny, transparent, and *soft.* In more informal contexts, the speaker may also choose to use somewhat less "academic" but more colorful adjectives such as *slimy, gigantic, bumpy,* and *fluffy.*

Choose an object from your area of studies and in the space that follows write down some words that describe the object or some of its parts. Share them with a partner.

Statements of Purpose

When describing an object, one of the speaker's goals is to explain the purpose or function of both the object and its parts, especially if the audience is unfamiliar with them. Take a body part, such as an eye. The general purpose of the eye may be known to the audience, but the purpose of the retina, cornea, and so on may not be. Two common ways to express purpose are by using

- A formal definition

- Terms that express purpose or function

Formal definitions

Formal definitions generally consist of three parts: the term (in this case, the object), the class the term belongs to, and the term's essential differences or distinguishing characteristics. One essential difference or distinguishing characteristic of an object may be its function or purpose. (See unit 4 for further discussion of formal definitions.)

Example:

		Essential differences/Distinguishing
Term	Class	characteristics (Function/Purpose)
↓	↓	↓

A bar code is *an electronic signal that's used to track the product.*

Terms that express purpose or function

In addition to using a formal definition, there are a number of ways to express purpose in spoken academic English. Six are listed here.

Term	Examples
1. *Term* functions as + noun	1. *The cornea* functions as a protective cover for the lens.
2. The purpose (function) of *term* is to + verb (infinitive)	2. The purpose of *the cornea* is to protect the lens.
3. *Term(s)* + verb (present simple)	3. The *pedestal, pillar, and neck* (of the harp) provide the main support.
4. *Term* is used to + verb (infinitive)	4. *The pedals* are used to enhance the sound.
5. *Term* is for + verb + ing (gerund)	5. *The pins* are for tuning the strings.
6. What *term* does is (cleft-sentence with *what* + infinitive)*	6. What the *pedals* do is (to) enhance the sound

*See unit 3 "Supplementary Materials," p. 87, for another use of cleft sentences using *what*.

Organization Indicator Statements

When preparing your object speech, keep in mind that organization indicator statements can be an effective means of notifying the audience of upcoming information and how the information is likely to be organized. (See unit 1, p. 5.) For example, an organization indicator could be used to tell the audience

- How many major parts you have divided the object into

  Trees consist of three major parts—**the crown, the trunk, and the roots.**

- How many purposes of an object you will discuss

  The cornea has two main purposes. **One* is to . . . . The other* is. . .**

---

*See unit 5 for a discussion of listing connectors.

Making Visual Aids

For your presentation, you will need a transparency of the object you've chosen to describe. First, draw or trace the object or take a picture of the object from another source, such as a magazine, textbook, encyclopedia, software package, or the Web (e.g., Google has a photo source). If you take a picture from another source, it may be necessary to modify it to suit your needs. Also, be sure to cite the source of the picture.

▧ Task 4

Look at the original source for the picture of the tree in task 2. Compare the two drawings. What modifications has the speaker made? How do these modifications make the visual aid more effective?

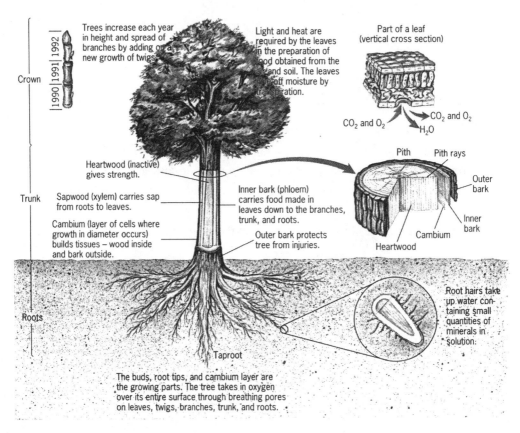

(From C. H. Stoddard, *Essentials of Forestry Practice,* 3d ed. [New York: John Wiley and Sons, 1978]. Copyright © 1978. Reprinted by permission of John Wiley and Sons, Inc.)

Tips for Enhancing Your Visual Aid

1. Make your visual aids attractive but simple. Quickly add color by using a transparency marker if you think it will enhance your visual aid. It is also possible to make attractive color transparencies, but they are sometimes more expensive. (See p. 41.)

2. Make your picture large and eye catching. Enlarge small pictures on a photocopier or on your computer before making your transparency. Make all lettering clear and large enough to read. If you wish, use Power Point or another available software package.

3. Remove all extraneous wording from your visual aid, including the names of parts you don't plan to discuss. However, don't forget to (1) provide a title, (2) label all major parts or components, and (3) include the source from which the visual aid was taken. You can use your word processor to help you.

To summarize, (1) make your visual aid attractive but simple, (2) use both a large image and clear, easy-to-read lettering, and (3) don't include extraneous written information, but do write a title, label the important parts, and provide the citation.

▨ Task 5

Take a look at the following visuals. What do you like about them? What, if anything, would you modify?

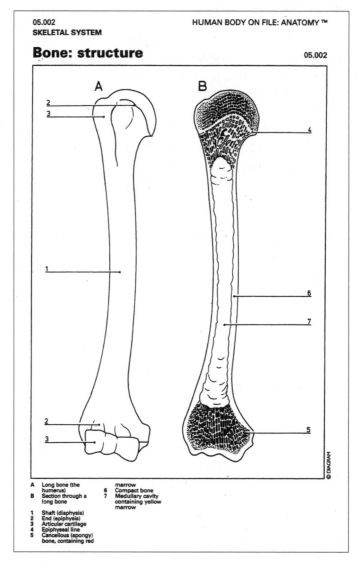

(From *Human Body on File: Anatomy*. Copyright © 1983 by Diagram Visual Information. Reprinted by permission of Facts On File, Inc.)

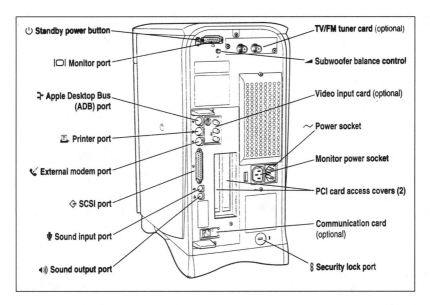

Ò Standby power button
|OI Monitor port
⊁ Apple Desktop Bus (ADB) port
⌨ Printer port
☏ External modem port
⬦ SCSI port
⇩ Sound input port
◀)) Sound output port

TV/FM tuner card (optional)
◄ Subwoofer balance control
Video input card (optional)
∼ Power socket
Monitor power socket
PCI card access covers (2)
Communication card (optional)
Security lock port

(From *Power Macintosh User's Manual,* 1997 Apple Computer, Inc. Reprinted by permission of Apple Computer, Inc.)

Making a Transparency

One way to make a transparency from a photocopy of your visual aid is to use a photocopier and a blank transparency.* Generally these are available in your department or at a photocopy shop. If you wish to make the transparency yourself, be sure to follow instructions for the specific photocopier you plan to use. If someone is making the transparency for you, supply the person with a photocopy of your visual.

Another way to make a transparency is to use your printer. You will need to buy special transparencies for this. If you have a color printer, you should be able to make color transparencies.

---

*See unit 3, p. 75, for a discussion of computer projection.

■ Task 6: Preparing Your Presentation

To help you develop your speech, you may wish to quickly fill in the table that follows. First, write down the name of your object and its major parts. Then, if it's relevant, write down some words that usefully describe them. Think about shape, texture, color, taste, size, type, and so on. Finally, write down the purpose(s) or function(s) of both the object and its major parts. After you have finished, decide what organizational strategy you will use to introduce the parts.

Object	Descriptive words	Function(s)/purpose(s)
Parts		

Organizational strategy/strategies:

Checking for Understanding

When you give a presentation, some members of the audience may have problems understanding you. For example, if you mispronounce key vocabulary words, speak too softly or quickly, or choose a topic that is too technical, you may "lose your audience." Pause during your speech to check for understanding. Here are some expressions used in actual academic settings to check for understanding.

1. Everybody understand?*

2. Does everybody understand . . . ?

3. So did everyone understand that?**

4. You understand?*

5. You understand that?*

6. Is that clear? Is that okay?

7. Is that clear? No? Yes?

8. Are you following here?**

9. Everyone understand?*

10. You following?*

11. Is this clear?

12. Are you with me?

▓ Task 7: Presentation

1. For homework prepare a five- to six-minute presentation in which you describe an object from your area of studies. Consider choosing an object that the audience is familiar with but does not know much about. If your area of studies focuses on abstract concepts, you may wish to describe a standard written text commonly used in your field, such as a contract, standard form, case study, or stock report.

---

*Notice that the speaker has omitted the auxiliary.
**That and here likely refer to something the speaker has just said.
Examples 1–10 are taken from MICASE 2000.

Do not discuss a process or problem plus solution for this speech. They are different speech types and will be discussed later in the text. If you are in doubt about your topic, discuss it with your instructor.

2. Think about your audience. What characteristics of the audience are relevant for this speech? Ask yourself questions such as, "Is my topic too difficult or easy for this audience?"

3. Keep your time limit in mind. If your object has a large number of parts, focus only on the major parts and eliminate the others.

4. Place your object in a larger context. Give adequate background information about the object and discuss its importance. Define it, if necessary, by using a formal three-part definition or terms that express purpose or function.

5. Choose an organizational strategy (or strategies) that suits the object you will describe.

6. Think about the language you will use to introduce or point to the object and its parts and move from one part to the next.

7. Choose words that will enhance the description of your object.

8. When explaining the function of the object or its parts, use a formal definition or terms that express purpose or function.

9. Make a transparency of the object. You generally need only one transparency for your speech. Make sure that (1) the visual has a title and that the important parts are labeled, (2) both the picture and lettering are large and clear, and (3) all unnecessary writing is eliminated. Use Power Point if you wish. Keep in mind that if you spend too much time preparing your visual aid, you may not have enough time to devote to your speech. If you prefer to bring a real object, be prepared to use the blackboard to write key terms.

10. Practice your speech out loud and standing, three or four times. The last time, record it using an audio- or videotape. Listen to your speech and decide what sections need improvement. Use the Object Speech Evaluation Form as a guide. Then practice it several more times. Critique your nonverbal behavior too.

11. Before you give your speech, decide where you will stop to make sure that the audience is following you. Rely on the expressions in "Checking for Understanding" on page 43 to help you.

Prespeech Evaluation

After practicing your speech several times, record it and then fill in the following self-evaluation form.

Object Speech Evaluation Form				
Name: _____				
	(Make a check in the appropriate column)			
	Good	OK	Needs Work	Comments (include specific problems you noticed)
Object Interesting? Appropriate for the audience?				
Introduction Clear? Placed object in a larger context? Gave a definition and some background information? Pointed out object's importance?				
Organization Chose an effective organizational strategy? Used an organization indicator statement(s)?				
Pointing words and spatial connectors suitable for Introducing the object? Pointing out its parts? Moving on to a subsequent part? Relating the parts to each other?				
Gestures Hands were free to point at the object? Gestures were expressive?				
Purpose Clearly explained the purpose or function of the object and its parts?				

	(Make a check in the appropriate column)			
	Good	OK	Needs Work	Comments (include specific problems you noticed)
Conclusion Smooth? Reiterated the importance of the object?				
Visual aid (transparency) Large and clear? Properly labeled? Unnecessary writing eliminated? Citation included?				
Pace Not too fast or too slow? Smooth rather than hesitant, choppy?				
Interaction with audience Friendly, approachable speaker? Good eye contact (looked at all the listeners)? Checked to see if listeners were understanding? Strong, confident voice?				

Pronunciation

(specific problems)

Other comments

Goals for my next presentation (list 2–3 areas that you want to improve on for your next presentation)

Final Evaluation

Listen to your final speech. Then, fill in the Object Speech Evaluation Form. Be sure to provide specific comments in the "comments" section. Also, set goals for your next speech.

If you would like to evaluate your speech with one or two partners, together discuss your strengths and weaknesses and then fill in the final Object Speech Evaluation Form. If you wish, include feedback from your partners on the form.

Object Speech Evaluation Form

Name: _____

	(Make a check in the appropriate column)			
	Good	OK	Needs Work	Comments (include specific problems you noticed)
Object Interesting? Appropriate for the audience?				
Introduction Clear? Placed object in a larger context? Gave a definition and some background information? Pointed out object's importance?				
Organization Chose an effective organizational strategy? Used an organization indicator statement(s)?				
Pointing words and spatial connectors suitable for Introducing the object? Pointing out its parts? Moving on to a subsequent part? Relating the parts to each other?				
Gestures Hands were free to point at the object? Gestures were expressive?				
Purpose Clearly explained the purpose or function of the object and its parts?				

	(Make a check in the appropriate column)			
	Good	OK	Needs Work	Comments (include specific problems you noticed)
Conclusion Smooth? Reiterated the importance of the object?				
Visual aid (transparency) Large and clear? Properly labeled? Unnecessary writing eliminated? Citation included?				
Pace Not too fast or too slow? Smooth rather than hesitant, choppy?				
Interaction with audience Friendly, approachable speaker? Good eye contact (looked at all the listeners)? Checked to see if listeners were understanding? Strong, confident voice?				

Pronunciation
(specific problems)

Other comments

Goals for my next presentation (list 2–3 areas that you want to improve on for your next presentation)

Unit 2 Supplementary Materials

Pronunciation: Stress

As discussed in unit 1, improper pausing places extra demands on listeners and may make a presentation seem choppy and hesitant or unnaturally fast-paced. Another pronunciation problem that can interfere with listeners' comprehension is improper stress or emphasis. In English, words that provide information to the listener, such as nouns, adjectives, verbs, and adverbs, are generally stressed. If these key words are left unstressed, the listener may not hear valuable information. Less important words that carry little information, such as articles *(the, a, an),* prepositions *(in, at),* and pronouns (e.g., *he, she, it*), are generally not stressed unless the speaker purposely highlights them. If these words are mistakenly stressed, they may misinform the listeners as to which are the key words in the sentence.

Speakers who fail to stress words that occur at the ends of sentences may find it even more difficult to convey their message. This is because in English new information generally occurs further on in the sentence. If listeners can't hear new information, they may lose the drift of what the speaker is saying. Look at the following sentence from the introduction of an object speech.

This is a harp.

Clearly, *harp* is the most important word in the sentence. The speaker is probably introducing the topic of his speech. If a key word isn't stressed and consequently the listeners don't hear it, they will have to rely on their eyes (i.e., viewing a picture or the object itself) and contextual cues to decipher it.

How does stress help the listener? When the speaker stresses a word, s/he speaks louder. As a result, the word takes longer to say. This makes it easier for the listener to hear it. Unstressed words, on the other hand, are said more quickly.

What does the speaker actually stress? If the word has only one syllable, such as *harp,* the whole word is stressed.

This is a HARP.

If the word has two syllables, such as *guitar,* one syllable is generally stressed and the other unstressed. In the case of *guitar,* the second syllable is stressed.

This is a gui/TAR.

However, sometimes both syllables are stressed, one with heavier, or primary, stress (´) and the other with lighter, or secondary, stress (`), as in *trombone*.

This is a TRÒM/BÓNE.

In words with three or more syllables, two syllables may also be stressed, one with primary stress (´) and the other with secondary stress (`). One example is the word *violin*. There is generally secondary stress on the first syllable, primary stress on the last syllable. But the middle syllable is left unstressed (˘).

This is a VÌ/ŏ/LÍN.

How does a speaker know which syllables to stress? If you look in a good English dictionary, the stressed syllables of all words are marked (except words with only one syllable). Alternative pronunciations are also listed. Word stress may vary with different dialects of English. This can initially cause comprehension problems for listeners that the speaker should be aware of.

Task 8

With other members of your class, look at the following sentences from a short speech. Underline the key words (especially nouns, verbs, adjectives, and adverbs) that you think convey information to the listeners. A good strategy for doing this is to first identify the new information the speaker introduces in each sentence. With the help of your instructor, add stress marks over the syllables that receive primary and secondary stress. Avoid stressing unimportant words; otherwise, it will be more difficult for the audience to understand your message fully. When you finish, say each sentence, using the stress marks that you have added.

This is a harp. ////

The harp is a stringed instrument // with a large triangular frame made of wood. ////

The most important part of the frame is this column. // It provides the main support for the harp. ////

The column consists of a pedestal, a pillar, and a neck. ////

These are the strings. ////

They're made of metal and create the harp's unique sound. ////

▓ Task 9

Listen to a tape of your object speech and write down five or six sentences. Underline each word that you stressed and indicate which syllable(s) of the word you stressed the loudest ('). Did you stress too many or too few words? Make corrections and practice saying those sentences again.

Giving a Tour

Getting oriented to an academic community includes becoming familiar with its facilities, which include areas in which departmental units are housed, libraries, computer centers, museums, laboratories, sports facilities, the health service, the student union, and other prominent sites. These spaces tell us much about academic life and the unique physical requirements of different areas of academic study. When you first arrive at the university, you will hear descriptions of these facilities. Later you may be called on to describe the same facilities to others who are unfamiliar with them. For example, you may find yourself giving a tour of your department to a new colleague or explaining the layout of a laboratory to a group of undergraduate students.

In addition to describing facilities on campus, if you are in a field such as business, history, engineering, architecture, archaeology, natural sciences, law, or urban planning, you may have the opportunity to describe areas off campus related to your field of studies, such as historical, architectural, and engineering sites, natural areas, traditional or innovative floor layouts, or street plans.

In this speech, which is designed to be used as an alternative to describing an object, you will give a virtual tour of a physical space, using a site plan. You can choose a facility on campus, an area related to your field of studies, or a site that you yourself have created as part of your academic work.

▨ Task 10

In groups, look at one of the two floor plans that follow and discuss the following questions.

1. Before you began a tour of this space, what would you say to set the scene?

2. Where would you start the tour?

3. How would you organize the tour? What organizational strategy (strategies) would you use?

4. What parts of the floor plan would you highlight on your tour? What parts would you eliminate? Why?

5. What specific information might the audience want to know about the most important parts of the site?

6. List some expressions used in English to explain the location of a particular area in the facility or its relationship to other areas, such as

    As you turn right, you'll see . . .

    Next to the . . . is the X.

    Over in the corner behind the X . . .

    On the second floor, you have . . .

    Directly in front of the X is the Y.

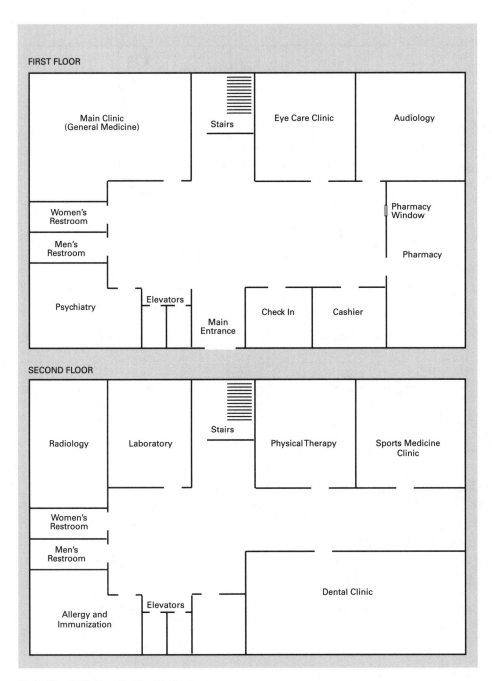

Floor Plan 1: University Health Center

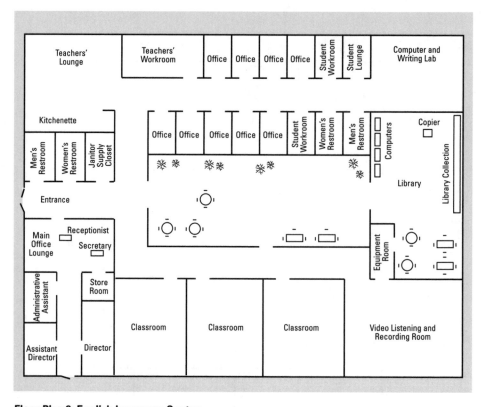

Floor Plan 2: English Language Center

▓ Task 11

Task 11 is an alternative to task 10. With your class or individually, visit a facility at your university chosen by your instructor. Using an available floor plan, visit the different areas of the site indicated on the plan. Circle the areas that you would highlight on a tour. Later, in groups, discuss the same questions as those posed in task 10.

1. Before you began a tour of this space, what would you say to set the scene?

2. Where would you start the tour?

3. How would you organize the tour? What organizational strategy (strategies) would you use?

4. What parts of the floor plan would you highlight on your tour? What parts would you eliminate? Why?

5. What specific information might the audience want to know about the most important parts of the site?

6. List some expressions used in English to explain the location of a particular area in the facility and/or its relationship to other areas, such as

> *As you turn right, you'll see . . .*
>
> *Next to the . . . is the X.*
>
> *Over in the corner behind the X . . .*
>
> *On the second floor, you have . . .*
>
> *Directly in front of the X is the Y.*

Planning Your Tour

Choose a space that you would like to give a tour of. Think about how you will design your tour. Planning involves a number of strategies. Go over the following recommendations with your instructor. Because there are similarities between giving a tour and describing an object, references to relevant information covered in the first part of the unit are listed below.

1. Place the site you've chosen in a context. Provide some background information about the site, such as

   - The general location of the site

   - The date the site was constructed and the original purpose of the site

   - The current function(s) of the present site

2. Develop an organizational strategy for introducing the parts of the site. For example, you may wish to discuss the parts spatially, beginning with the part closest to the main entrance. Or you can discuss the most important parts first and the least important parts last. You could also discuss the parts logically, stressing the relationship between various parts. Or you may wish to use more than one strategy. (See "Organization" on pp. 30–31 in this unit.)

3. Use various verbal strategies for pointing out locations on your tour. (Carefully review "Pointing with Words" on page 34 in this unit for

common ways to introduce and locate objects in English.) Relate one location to another by using demonstrative pronouns, such as *this* and *that;* location prepositions, such as *(right) next to, (directly) behind, in front of, overhead, underneath, to the right of the door, in the basement;* the adverbs *here* and *there;* and adverbial clauses such as *as you go in the front door.*

4. Discuss the function or purpose of the major areas on your tour. (On pp. 36–37, see the section "Statements of Purpose," on formal definitions and terms that express function or purpose, for ways in English to express the function of an object.)

5. An object is generally introduced with the article *a* or *an,* as in *This is a receipt.* However, a site is considered to be unique and thus is often introduced by its name, such as *Hopkins Hall* or *Ellis Island.* Sometimes the name includes the article *the,* as in *the student union, the health center, the music library.* It tells the listener that there is only one such building. An exception is if there are two or more structures, such as two or more computer labs that are similar, as in *This is a typical computer lab in the School of Public Health. The* is used the same way to introduce the parts of a site as to introduce the parts of an object. (See p. 34.)

Task 12: Alternate Presentation

1. Give a five- or six-minute virtual tour of one of the following: a facility on your university campus, an interesting building or area related to your field of studies, or a site that you yourself have designed.

2. When planning your speech, take into account the suggestions discussed in "Planning Your Tour" above.

3. Use a transparency. If a site plan is already available, it will save you time. Otherwise, make a simple site plan. Clearly label the areas you will discuss and eliminate unnecessary writing.

4. Use strategies for keeping in touch with the audience, including a friendly, approachable demeanor, good eye contact, a strong, confident voice, and expressive gestures. Also, choose places in your speech to stop and check if the audience is understanding.

5. Practice your speech two or three times. Then, record it. Listen to your speech and decide which sections need improvement. Use the pre-speech evaluation form to critique your performance, including your non-verbal behavior.

Prespeech Evaluation: Tour Speech

Name: _____

After practicing your speech several times, use the following questions to evaluate your final presentation.

1. Was your topic appropriate and interesting for the audience?

2. How did you set the scene?

3. What organizational strategy (strategies) did you use?

4. What verbal strategies did you use for pointing out locations on your tour (e.g., *as you turn right, you'll see; here you have*)?

5. Was your speech too short or too long? Did you highlight too many or too few areas? What changes would you make?

6. How did you express the purpose or function of important areas?

7. Did you develop a positive relationship with the audience by

   • adopting a friendly, approachable demeanor,

   • establishing good eye contact,

   • using expressive gestures, and

   • checking to see if the audience was following you?

Final Evaluation: Tour Speech

Name: _____

Listen to your final speech. Then, fill in the evaluation form. If you would like to evaluate your speech with one or two partners, together discuss your strengths and weaknesses and then fill in the form. You may wish to include feedback from your partners on the form.

1. Was your topic appropriate and interesting for the audience?

2. How did you set the scene?

3. What organizational strategy (strategies) did you use?

4. What verbal strategies did you use for pointing out locations on your tour (e.g., *as you turn right, you'll see; here you have*)?

5. Was your speech too short or too long? Did you highlight too many or too few areas? What changes would you make?

6. How did you express the purpose or function of important areas?

7. Did you develop a positive relationship with the audience by

    • adopting a friendly, approachable demeanor,

    • establishing good eye contact,

    • using expressive gestures, and

    • checking to see if the audience was following you?

Unit 3

Explaining a Process or Procedure

Members of all academic disciplines work with processes or procedures. Students and faculty may be expected to explain, discover, create, implement, modify, or follow processes or procedures as part of their training or professional responsibilities. *Processes* are generally viewed as a progression or series of events, steps, or changes that have a beginning and end or end result. However, some processes are cyclical or continuing. Processes can be natural or can involve human intervention. Established processes for carrying out specific tasks are generally referred to as *procedures*.

Speeches about processes can be organized in various ways, depending on the purpose of the speech. For example, if we want to highlight several recent improvements on a process, we may simply enumerate the modifications using listing as the main organizational strategy. However, if our purpose is to explain a process, we will generally focus on the chronological dimension of the process and will choose chronological order as the main organizational strategy. In this unit, this chronological dimension will be emphasized.

In academic English, it can be more challenging to explain a process than to describe a single object. Technical processes may involve not just one but several objects, such as a set of tools, as well as the materials and people needed to carry them out. This is the case, for example, when an engineer describes how concrete is made, a professor of film and video studies explains a film-editing procedure, or an ecology student discusses a new process for removing pollutants from the soil. Both natural processes that take place without human intervention and procedures that primarily involve the actions of people rather than objects and materials can be complex, especially if they include a number of relationships and events. This is the case, for example, when a geologist describes the process of soil formation or a law student explains how a legal case goes through the court system. Therefore, presenters need to plan their speeches carefully. For example, they have to decide what background information the audience needs to know before presenting the process, what terms may be unfamiliar to the audience and when to introduce and explain them, and what strategies for presenting the steps in the process will enhance listeners' comprehension and interaction.

For your next presentation, you will explain a process or procedure from your field of studies. Since you will be speaking to a general academic audience and will have time constraints, your presentation can be neither too simple nor too long and complex. Write down several processes related to your field of studies. As you go through the exercises in this unit, evaluate these processes as possible final presentation topics.

Task 1

Look at the following information on a transparency*. What procedure has the speaker chosen to discuss?

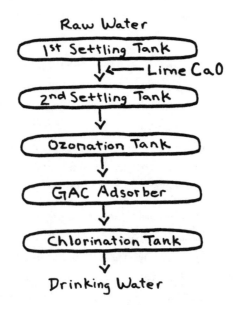

Now answer the questions.

Discussion Questions

1. What is the topic of this process speech? Do you think it is appropriate for a general academic audience? Would you personally be interested in listening to this speech? What might it depend on?

2. Approximately how many steps does the speaker discuss? How can you tell? What organization indicator statement (see unit 1, p. 5 and unit 2, p. 37) could the speaker use to introduce the steps?

---

*Based on a student drawing.

3. What information does the speaker include in her transparency? Do you think the speech would be more effective if the speaker wrote out each step on the transparency? Why or why not?

4. What are some of the terms that the speaker will likely define during her speech? Is she more likely to explain these terms in the introduction or as she explains the process?

5. Compare the speaker's first transparency with the second one she made, shown below. How has she improved the transparency? Can you think of other ways of making the transparency more eye-catching?

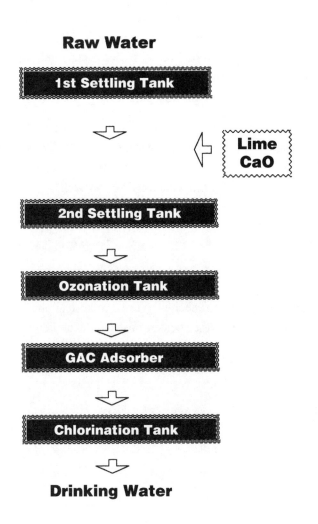

The topic of this speech appears to be well chosen. It is relevant to a general academic audience because it relates to our daily lives. However, if the speech is too simple, the speaker will lose the attention of the audience. Therefore, she will want to make her speech as informative as possible without making it so technical that the audience won't understand.

The speaker's first transparency is adequate. It is neat and clearly labeled. There is room to write additional information during the delivery. However, it is not particularly eye-catching. Her second version is more attractive. The speaker has chosen bolder lettering and more decorative borders. Color can be cheaply and easily added to a transparency by using a transparency marker. Color transparencies can also be made by using a color printer and special transparencies or a color photocopier and a color picture.

It is obvious from the transparency that the speaker will describe five main steps in the water purification process. However, the transparency does not indicate what these steps are, only where they take place. This may be an advantage. The transparency still provides an outline for both the class and the speaker to follow. But, since there is little writing on the transparency the audience's attention remains on the speaker and not the transparency.

The speaker will likely have to explain the words on her transparency that indicate where stages in the process take place, such as *settling tank, ozonation tank,* and *GAC adsorber.* She may prefer to do this when she discusses the relevant stage, rather than during the introduction of the speech.

Introductions to Process Speeches

1. Using rhetorical questions

One way to begin a process speech is to use a rhetorical question. Rhetorical questions are questions that the speaker poses to the audience but that don't require an answer.

Task 2

Look at the following introduction and identify any rhetorical questions. In what sentence does the speaker introduce the topic?

> (1) Have you ever thought about where the water you drink comes from?
>
> (2) Many times it comes from rivers and lakes that have contaminated water. (3) How is this water purified so that it is safe for you to drink?
>
> (4) Today, I'm going to explain a process commonly used to purify drinking water.

Rhetorical questions are an effective means of opening the speech for the following reasons.

- Rhetorical questions are more apt to get the audience's attention than an opener like *Today I'm going to talk about . . .*

- Rhetorical questions gradually lead the audience into the topic of the speech, and thus may more effectively guarantee that the audience is following the speaker.

- By using rhetorical questions, the speaker begins a relationship with the audience that can be maintained throughout the speech.

One drawback to using rhetorical questions is that the audience may think that some questions are real and that the speaker is asking the audience to answer them. One way speakers solve this problem is by not pausing long enough for the audience to respond.

2. Providing background information

Before getting too far into an explanation of the process, the speaker usually needs to give necessary background information. The introduction may include such information as

- The definition of the process

- The purpose of the process (if it is not included in the definition)

- Other important definitions

- Equipment and material used in the process

- The people involved in the process

- The number of steps in the process

■ Task 3

First, look at the following introduction to a presentation on the Rankine cycle. Then, working with a partner, put a check (✓) before the introduction strategies the speaker used from the following list:

— 1. A rhetorical question

— 2. A definition of the process

— 3. The purpose(s) of the process

— 4. Other important definitions or explanation of terms

— 5. Material used in the process

— 6. Equipment used in the process

— 7. People involved in the process

— 8. The number of steps in the process

How does the speaker begin his speech? What rhetorical question might the speaker have begun with instead?

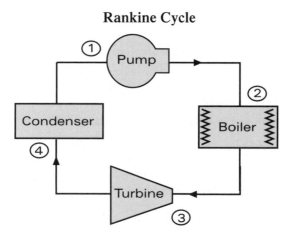

Rankine Cycle

Rankine Cycle

1. Good morning, everyone.

2. Today, I'd like to talk about a basic thermal cycle usually used in a power plant. It is called Rankine cycle.

3. Before I launch into the introduction of the Rankine cycle, I would like to explain what a thermal cycle means first. Simply speaking, a thermal cycle is a cycle which is related to some thermodynamic property change, such as temperature, pressure, or density.

4. Okay, now let's go back to the Rankine cycle. Basically the cycle is composed of four steps, as you can see in the figure. The working fluid usually used is is water. And the working fluid here experiences all the steps inside the cycle.

In the introduction to his speech, the speaker successfully (1) introduces the process he is going to describe (the Rankine cycle) and defines it, (2) explains terms *(thermal cycle* and *thermodynamic property change)* that the audience may need to understand the process, (3) states the number of steps in the process (four) by using an organization indicator statement, and (4) tells the audience the material used in the process (water).

Task 4

Finish reading the speech on the Rankine cycle aloud with your partner. Look at the speaker's visual aid as you read. Answer the questions that follow.

5. Now let's follow the flow direction of the fluid to see how this cycle works.

6. At the beginning, the liquid is pumped into the boiler by a pump, and then inside the boiler the liquid is heated into a vapor.

7. In the boiler, the liquid reaches a high temperature and high pressure, which means the energy level is increased. This is also the function of the boiler—to increase the energy level of the working fluid so that the fluid can do works.

8. You'll see how this working fluid does the work in the next step. Now let's move to the next step.

9. The high-pressure, high-temperature vapor moves to the turbine to drive the generators and generate electricity.

10. And after going through this turbine, the working fluid is cooled down, which means the energy level is reduced. Why the energy level is reduced is because some of the energy is used to drive the generator. That means the working fluid is doing some work.

11. Okay, then after this step, the cooled vapor travels to a condenser and inside the condenser, the vapor is condensed to a liquid again, so that the cycle can be repeated again and again.

12. Now that's is my brief introduction to how the Rankine cycle works.

(Presentation by Jr-Hung Tsai, with minor changes.)

Discussion Questions

1. What are the four steps in the Rankine cycle?

2. What is the purpose of *let's* in sections 4, 5, and 8?

3. What time connectors does the speaker use to move from one step to another?

4. What verb tense does the speaker use to describe the steps in the process?

5. Does the speaker generally use active or passive voice?

Organizing the Process: Linking Words

As long as your introduction contains the necessary background information, you should have few problems organizing the main part of the speech, the explanation of the process. This is because the process mainly involves sequential steps (several single steps that occur one after the other). However, don't overlook the importance of linking words (signposts) to move from one step of your process to another.

Let's

The expression *Let's* is commonly used by speakers to inform the listeners of a transition to a new topic or subtopic. In the "Rankine Cycle" speech, the speaker effectively uses it to tell the listeners that he is going on to a new step in the process (*Now let's follow the flow direction of the fluid* [section 5], *Now let's move to the next step* [section 8]). However, he also uses *Now let's* to provide a smooth transition back to the process after he interrupts it to introduce the definition of *thermal cycle* (*Now let's go back to the Rankine cycle* [section 4]).

Let's (Let us), by definition, includes the audience. Therefore, using it in your presentation can be one way to enhance your relationship with the audience.

Time Connectors

In unit 1 you used time connectors in your introduction speeches to link sequences of events from past to present. The presenter of the "Rankine Cycle" speech also uses time connectors such as *at the beginning, and then, after going through this turbine,* and *then after this step* to explain the chronological relationships between the steps in the process and to help inform the audience that the speaker is moving on to the next step of the process. For these reasons, the connectors are generally found at the beginning of the utterance.

Explaining the Process: Tense, Voice, the Imperative (Command)

Tense

Present tense is generally used to explain a process, especially if the process is a standard procedure or a predictable or recurring event. If you look at the "Rankine Cycle" speech, you will see that the speaker chooses present tense throughout (e.g., the liquid *is pumped,* the liquid *is heated,* the vapor *moves* to the turbine, the cooled vapor *travels* to a condenser, the vapor *is condensed*). If, however, a speaker chooses to explain a procedure that s/he specifically carried out (e.g., as part of a research study), then the past tense is useful. In this case, *I* or *we* can generally be used as the subject.

Voice

Whether the speaker uses active or passive voice depends primarily on how the action is carried out.

Passive voice: The speaker generally uses passive voice when an action is carried out by "an actor" such as a person, machine, or another outside force. The focus of the speech is on the process, not the actor (e.g., the liquid *is pumped,* the liquid *is heated,* the vapor *is condensed*). So, by using passive voice, the speaker is able to place the topic or current focus in subject position, which is customary in English, and de-emphasize or even eliminate the actor altogether (the water *is tested* for contaminants).

Active voice: If the process itself is a natural one, active voice is commonly used (e.g., when the rain *falls* to the ground, the vapor *moves* to the turbine). Active voice can also be used to de-emphasize outside intervention (e.g., as the boxes *travel* along the conveyer belt; cf. the boxes *are moved* along the conveyer belt). In this case, it's as if the process is being viewed as a natural one. Active voice may have been chosen for its simplicity or economy.

Active voice may also be used if there are several key players in a procedure, and the speaker needs to clarify the roles of each. In the following example from civil law, the use of the passive would be awkward.

The *judge* instructs the jury on what law to apply in the case. The *jury* applies the law and decides the outcome of the case. *Both parties* have the right to appeal the decision of the jury.

The imperative (command)

The imperative or command form is commonly used in a process speech when the speaker wishes to instruct the listeners on how to carry out a task. Giving instructions is far more frequent in some university contexts than others and may take place under more informal circumstances rather than during more formal academic events. Laboratory assistants, art and music instructors, and dental and nursing students may find giving instructions part of their regular work with colleagues and clients. In these cases, there may be more interaction between the speaker and the listener(s).

It is common in spoken English to include *you* when using the imperative (*Stand* or *You stand* with your arms around the victim's waist). Depending on how it's used, *you* followed by a verb could also be considered a statement rather than a command. *You* can also be followed by a modal, such as *have to* or *will. You* need not refer to a specific individual or group of individuals but can be used to refer to people in general. (See "How to Help Someone Who Is Choking" in the "Supplementary Materials" in this unit on pp. 85–86.)

Passive Voice	Active Voice	Imperative (Command)
The process is generally carried out by a person, machine, or another outside force (outside intervention).	1. The process is viewed as a natural one. 2. The speaker wishes to de-emphasize intervention by an outside force. 3. There are several key players in the process, each with important roles.	The speaker gives instructions for the audience to follow.
Examples: *After the first step is complete, lime is added to the water.* *Finally, the rocket is drawn to earth by gravity.* (Notice that *lime* and *rocket* are in subject position because they are the topic or speaker's current focus. New information follows. (Cf. *Finally gravity draws the rocket to earth*, which would change the topic/focus to *gravity*.)	Examples: *Acid rain falls on the soil. . . .* *The water flows from the first tank to the second. (Cf. The water is pumped from the first tank to the second.)* *The judge chooses the instructions, but the jury applies them to the case at hand.*	Examples: *Stand with your arms around the victim's waist.* *You make a fist with one hand.* *You have to put your fist under the rib cage.* (Notice that *you* can refer to the listener or to anyone who carries out the process.)

Look at section 10 of the "Rankine Cycle" speech again. Do you think the speaker meant to say the working fluid *is cooled down* (passive voice), which would indicate that there was an outside force? Or do you think the speaker views the process as a natural one and meant to use active voice instead *(the working fluid cools down)*?

Task 5

With a partner, read the following two excerpts from the Michigan Corpus of Academic Spoken English (MICASE) at the English Language Institute, University of Michigan. For each passage, determine whether the verbs in bold are active, passive, the imperative, or *you* followed by a verb. Talk about why the speaker made these choices.

1. Oceanography lecture

Now let's talk a little bit about each of these types of sediment. And we'll start with the terrigenous, stuff. It's very difficult. To carry sediment, out into the ocean very far, if you think about it, what happens? The the rivers **flow down** to the ocean right? In general in most places not every place but in most places, as the river **comes down** from the mountains down through the hills down through the coastal plain, the level or the steepness of the slope of the river **gets** lower and lower, and then when the river **hits** the ocean, in a way it's like hitting a s— a rock wall. I mean that it can't go any deeper than that, and so the flow **stops**, in terms of river flow. And other processes take over. Currents, tidal flushing in and out, longshore currents, wave generated currents, things like that, **will** then **take** that sediment that's delivered by the rivers, and **move** it around a little bit.

2. Office hour discussion in statistics

Ten is not a reasonable value according to the interval right? Okay so we probably are going to what? End up rejecting or accepting? What do we think? Probably rejecting. All it requires us to do is to adjust our test statistic a little bit. You're gonna calculate, or you already have calculated X-bar and Y-bar, but you wanna now see whether difference in the sample means is significantly different from ten, okay? Significantly higher than ten so you're gonna **subtract** off ten instead of subtracting off zero. And then still **divide** by that standard error. That's your test statistic now. And you **do** the test the same way you would with any other two observed test statistics. Its degrees of freedom will be the thirteen degrees of freedom, and you've done the test so you just **adjust** what you subtract off as the hypothesized value.

(From MICASE 2000. Modifications have been made to make the transcripts easier to read.)

Using Modals in Process Speeches

When you are giving your process speech, you may find yourself using modals such as

must
should
have to
will

Modals are often unnecessary in process speeches if the speaker's goal is to explain rather than to instruct, train, admonish, or warn.* If the steps in the process are generally repeatable, predictable, standard, or intrinsic to the process, you can likely reduce the use of modals to streamline your explanation. However, if modals in some way clarify or enhance your explanation, you may wish to include them.

▓ Task 6

Look at the following steps taken from several different process speeches. Each contains a modal. Decide if the modal serves a useful purpose. If not, remove it.

1. First, the water has to be pumped into the boiler.

2. Then an incision will be made with a scalpel, which is a small knife with a sharp, thin blade.

3. First, the goals of the project should be clarified. Then, information about the potential site needs to be collected.

4. The building plan must be approved by the housing council before work begins.

▓ Task 7

Bring to class a visual representation of a process that you're thinking about using for your final presentation. Be prepared to discuss the following questions with your group.

1. What is the topic of the speech? Is it suitable for a general academic audience?

2. How you would open a speech on this topic with a rhetorical question?

---

* If your purpose is to instruct or warn, then you may find it useful to use modals such as *should, might want to, must, have to,* or *will.*

3. What background information would you include before beginning the process?

4. What tense and voice are appropriate for this topic?

5. What words might you define in your introduction? What words might you define as you explain the steps in the process?

■ Task 8: Preparing Your Presentation

To help you prepare your speech, quickly fill in the table that follows. What opener will you use? What background information do you need to present to the audience before you describe the steps in the process? Will you use an organization indicator statement to introduce the steps? What connectors will you use to move from one step to another?

Process:
Opener (possible rhetorical question):
Background information:
Steps or stages:

Checking for Understanding

When you give a presentation, some members of the audience may have problems understanding you. For example, if you mispronounce key vocabulary words, speak too softly or quickly, or choose a topic that is too technical, you may "lose your audience."

Below is the list of expressions used in academic settings to check for understanding. (See unit 2.)

In your last speech, how many times did you ask your listeners if they were following you? Did you use any of these expressions?

___ 1. Everybody understand?

___ 2. Does everybody understand . . . ?

___ 3. So did everyone understand that?

___ 4. You understand?

___ 5. You understand that?

___ 6. Is that clear? Is that okay?

___ 7. Is that clear? No? Yes?

___ 8. Are you following here?

___ 9. Everyone understand?

___ 10. You following?

___ 11. Is this clear?

___ 12. Are you with me?

___ 13. Other:

When planning your presentations, decide when you will pause to check for understanding. In your process speech, in which places could you break to check for understanding without greatly interrupting the flow of your speech? Mark appropriate breaks in the table in Task 8 above.

Examples 1–10 are taken from MICASE 2000.

Asking for Questions

At strategic points in your speech, it's also important to ask the audience if they have any questions. Questions serve the same purpose as the expressions listed above in "Checking for understanding"—to clear up uncertainties. In addition, your responses to questions from the audience can enrich your speech and enhance your relationship with the audience. Below are examples of ways speakers in academic settings elicit questions from the audience.

Task 9

Look at the examples and answer the following questions in your group.

- In which examples does the speaker tell the audience that s/he welcomes questions?
- In which examples does the speaker address a particular member of the audience?
- Look at examples 2, 3, and 4. Which of these can't be used at the end of a speech?
- In which example does the speaker indicate that there is not much time for questions?

Examples

1. You can ask questions at any time.
2. Any questions? Feel free to ask.*
3. Any questions before we move on?*
4. Any questions or comments so far?*
5. So, any questions on number 2 (on step 2)?*
6. If you have any questions, just raise your hand, it's okay.
7. I would be happy to entertain a few brief questions.
8. Ahmed, did you have a question?
9. Does anyone else have a question?
10. Any other questions, Ken?*
11. Any final questions?

Any questions? is commonly used to elicit questions from the audience. Notice that the auxiliary, subject, and verb *(Does anyone have)* are often omitted.
Examples 1–10 are from MICASE 2000. Words in parentheses have been added.

Tips on Using the Overhead Projector and the Blackboard

The following is a list of helpful tips for using both the OHP and the blackboard. As you plan your speech, envision how you will use one or both of these tools.

The overhead projector (OHP)

- Talk to the audience, not to the transparency. If possible, stand next to the screen, rather than the overhead projector (OHP), so that you and the audience can see each other better. As much as possible, keep your back to the screen and your eyes on the audience.

- If you have trouble gesturing naturally, standing at the screen can help you because as you speak, you can use your hand to refer to particular sections of your visual aid. If you stand next to the OHP, you may find it harder to gesture freely.

- Stand to one side of the OHP light or the other. The light is strong and can damage your eyes.

- If you have to stand next to the overhead projector to write on your visual aid, continue to make eye contact with the audience whenever possible. Also, try to gesture naturally.

- If you use several transparencies during your speech, place one on the overhead projector and the others on a table or cart near you. Don't hold them in your hand. Leave your hands free to gesture. Make sure your transparencies are in order before you begin your speech.

- If you want to show only part of your transparency to the audience at one time, cover the other parts with a piece of cardboard or paper. Or tape a piece of paper to the transparency.

The blackboard

- If you have to write a lot of information on the blackboard before your speech, your audience will become bored and you will use up your time allotment. You may also appear unprepared. Use a transparency instead.

- A blackboard can be beneficial for writing key terms, giving short explanations, or drawing simple illustrations. Plan how you will use the blackboard before your speech. During your speech, write clearly and quickly.

- Before you begin writing, make sure that the board is completely erased.

- Chalk can squeak if you hold it incorrectly. To avoid this annoyance, slant the chalk when you write and lighten the pressure.

- Talk to the audience, not to the blackboard. Even when writing, try to keep your back against the blackboard as much as possible. If you are right-handed, stand so that you can write toward yourself rather than away from yourself. If you are left-handed, do the opposite.

Should I use computer projection (an LCD player) instead of an overhead projector?

If you have access to computer projection, review the following information before deciding whether to use computer projection instead of an overhead projector (OHP).

1. Since all information is loaded on a disk, ready to project, computer projection may save the speaker time during a presentation.

2. If the speaker has one or two visual aids, it may be easier to make transparencies than set up and use computer projection equipment.

3. Transparencies for an OHP can be expensive. A computer projector is potentially cheaper to use. However, since a computer projector is more complex than an OHP, it is more likely that something will go wrong. The speaker may still need to prepare backup transparencies.

4. Computer projection makes nonlinear presentations possible. The speaker doesn't need to move from one image to another in a linear fashion but can skip quickly to the image s/he wants. Also, unlike the OHP, a computer projector can produce audio, video, and animation. These features help the speaker rethink how to present information. However, if images take up a lot of space, the speaker will need to have information on a Zip drive or hard drive.

5. If the speaker uses a transparency, s/he may have to manually cover up information on the transparency that s/he doesn't yet want the audience to see. With a computer projector, the speaker can feed information to the audience in a more attractive way.

6. Color presentations can be easily made using computer projection; however, computer projection doesn't guarantee accurate color. Presenters who require accurate colors may wish to consider using slides instead.

7. Computer projectors produce a better image if the presenter has control over the lighting in both the front and the back of the room.

8. If the computer projector has a remote control, the presenter has more flexibility in where s/he stands.

9. An eye-catching presentation using computer projection may still be criticized if it lacks such qualities as substance, a clear organizational strategy, a smooth flow, and audience consideration.

▨ Task 10: Presentation

1. Give a six- or seven-minute speech that describes a process in your field of studies. Choose a topic that interests a general academic audience that you can discuss within the time limit. If you choose a topic that is too technical or too simple, your audience will lose interest.

2. Include an attention-getting opening. Pose a rhetorical question to the listeners. Also ask yourself what background information the audience needs in order to understand the process.

3. Decide what time connectors you will use to make your speech easier for the audience to follow. Also try using the signpost *let's* as a linking word to connect steps in your process or return to your process after stopping to answer a question or define a term.

4. As you plan the steps in your process, ask yourself whether a step is best described using the active voice, passive voice, or both. Eliminate unnecessary modals. If you are giving a series of instructions, consider using commands (imperatives), *you* followed by a verb, and appropriate modals.

5. Plan to stop your speech at strategic breaks, such as at the end of your introduction or after a step, to ask the audience if they are following you or if they have any questions.

6. Before giving your speech, practice it at least two to three times. Then record it at least once on an audio- or videotape and evaluate yourself using the evaluation form on pages 78–79. Be sure to include a critique of your nonverbal behavior. Practice your presentation several more times.

7. Use a transparency to enhance your presentation. It will help you (1) maintain the audience's attention, (2) ensure that the audience is following you, and (3) remember what you are going to say. Before making your transparency, evaluate its effectiveness. Also ask another member of the class to evaluate it. Use the checksheet on page 77. If your partner answers *yes* to any of the questions, think how you might improve your visual aid.

8. Review the information presented in this unit on using the OHP, the blackboard, and computer projection. If you have access to computer projection, consider some of the advantages and disadvantages of using it instead of an OHP.

Visual Aid Self-Evaluation	Yes	No
1. Is it missing a title?		
2. Is any part of it too small to see?		
3. Are there marks or smudges?		
4. Have I forgotten to label important parts?		
5. Is it too cluttered or confusing?		
6. Does it have too much written information? Will the audience spend their time reading the visual aid instead of listening to me?		
7. Does it contain information that I don't plan to discuss?		

Evaluation of Partner's Visual Aid	Yes	No
1. Is it missing a title?		
2. Is any part of it too small to see?		
3. Are there marks or smudges?		
4. Have I forgotten to label important parts?		
5. Is it too cluttered or confusing?		
6. Does it have too much written information? Will the audience spend their time reading the visual aid instead of listening to the speaker?		
7. Does it contain information that the speaker doesn't plan to discuss?		

Prespeech Evaluation

Process Speech Evaluation Form

Name: _____

	(Make a check in the appropriate column)			
	Good	OK	Needs Work	Comments (include specific problems you noticed)
Topic Interesting process? Appropriate for a general academic audience?				
Introduction Used a rhetorical question or another attention-getting device? Provided useful background information before describing the process? Explained the relevance or importance of the process? Carefully organized introductory information?				
Process Clearly organized steps?				
Transitions Used time connectors and other signposts like *let's* to signal moves from one part of the process to another?				
Definitions Provided definitions of key terms that may have been unfamiliar to the audience?				
Grammar Used correct tense and voice to explain steps in the process or imperative if yours is an instructions speech? Used modals when they served a clear purpose?				

	(Make a check in the appropriate column)			
	Good	OK	Needs Work	Comments (include specific problems you noticed)
Pace Not too fast or slow? Smooth rather than hesitant, choppy?				
Eye contact Maintained eye contact with all listeners?				
Gestures Hands were free and expressive?				
Loudness Spoke loud enough for everyone to hear without straining?				
Interaction with audience Checked for understanding? Requested questions from the audience?				
Use of Equipment Used an OHP, the blackboard, or computer projection effectively?				

Pronunciation

(specific comments)

Other comments

Goals for my next presentation (list 2–3 areas that you want to improve on for your next presentation)

Final Evaluation

Process Speech Evaluation Form				

Name: _____

	(Make a check in the appropriate column)			
	Good	OK	Needs Work	Comments (include specific problems you noticed)
Topic Interesting process? Appropriate for a general academic audience?				
Introduction Used a rhetorical question or another attention-getting device? Provided useful background information before describing the process? Explained the relevance or importance of the process? Carefully organized introductory information?				
Process Clearly organized steps?				
Transitions Used time connectors and other signposts like *let's* to signal moves from one part of the process to another?				
Definitions Provided definitions of key terms that may have been unfamiliar to the audience?				
Grammar Used correct tense and voice to explain steps in the process or imperative if yours is an instructions speech? Used modals when they served a clear purpose?				

	(Make a check in the appropriate column)			
	Good	OK	Needs Work	Comments (include specific problems you noticed)
Pace Not too fast or slow? Smooth rather than hesitant, choppy?				
Eye contact Maintained eye contact with all listeners?				
Gestures Hands were free and expressive?				
Loudness Spoke loud enough for everyone to hear without straining?				
Interaction with audience Checked for understanding? Requested questions from the audience?				
Use of Equipment Used an OHP, the blackboard, or computer projection effectively?				

Pronunciation

(specific comments)

Other comments

Goals for my next presentation (list 2–3 areas that you want to improve on for your next presentation)

Unit 3 Supplementary Materials

Pronunciation: Intonation

In unit 1, pausing was defined as slowing down or coming to a complete stop at a particular point. Unit 2 discussed stress. Words that convey important information are stressed or said more forcefully in English. Speakers who use proper pausing and stress are able to convey their message more effectively.

Intonation also plays a key role in communicating information to the audience. Intonation is the rise and fall of the pitch of our voices as we speak. In English, speakers most frequently use midlevel pitch. When our intonation rises from mid level to high level, we are telling the listener that we have reached a word in the speech flow that we want to highlight.

In the following sentence, the speaker stresses the adjective, nouns, and verb in the sentence. In addition, the speaker highlights one word, *condenser,* by using a pattern of rising, then falling intonation. The intonation rises from mid level to high level on the stressed (second) syllable of *condenser,* and then falls to low level on the last, unstressed syllable before coming to a stop.

The **coo**led **va**por **tra**vels to a *condenser.* ////

This rising, falling intonation on the last word in the sentence is common in English. One reason is that new important information is usually found toward the end, rather than at the beginning, of the sentence in English.

If the sentence is longer and has more than one pause, rising and falling intonation may also occur on a highlighted word before each pause.

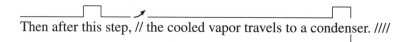

Then after this step, // the cooled vapor travels to a condenser. ////

Here the speaker uses rising intonation (from mid level to high level) twice, once on *this** and again on *condenser.* Since the speaker only slows down during the first pause, rather than coming to a complete stop, his intonation doesn't fall to low level but returns to mid level. This saves him the extra step of having to re-

---

*The speaker probably chooses to use rising intonation on *this,* because one of his main speech goals is to distinguish each step in the process.

turn to mid level from low level. Notice that sometimes there is a slight rise in intonation at this point.

In unit 1, we stated that one type of pausing involves coming to a full stop. The exercise marked full stops with //// at the end of each sentence. However, keep in mind that speaking is not like writing. In writing we put a period (full stop, as it is sometimes called) at the end of each sentence, but in speaking it isn't necessary to come to a full or complete stop. Instead, we can slow down. Compare these two sentences.

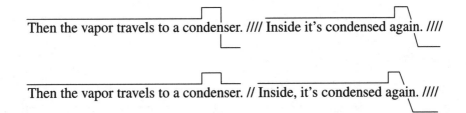

Notice that in the first example, the speaker pauses fully twice. When the speaker pauses fully (pause stop), his intonation falls to low level.

In the second example, the speaker only slows down when he reaches *condenser.* He doesn't stop. That is why his intonation falls to mid level, not to the low level. The first sentence seems to flow into the second sentence. This is one way presenters speak faster in English. However, if listeners have trouble understanding, they may be able to hear and absorb the information better if the speaker pauses fully.

As seen above, rising intonation can occur once or several times in a sentence. The word(s) on which it occurs can change, depending on the speaker. Compare these examples:

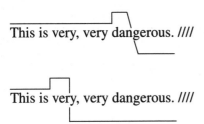

■ Task 11

Practice saying the paragraph from unit 1. Use rising intonation and then return to mid level or low level where indicated.*

This year, // John's studying business at the University of Michigan. ////

His major is management. // He hopes to manage a nonprofit corporation after he graduates. ////

Before John went to college, he traveled around the world for two years. ////

■ Task 12

Write down four sentences from the recording of your process speech. Mark the stress and intonation pattern you used. If you wish to alter your stress and intonation pattern, make adjustments and then practice the same four sentences again. Record the sentences and compare them with your first recording.

---

* // = slow down, //// = stop

Giving an Instructions Speech

The topic of the following instructions speech, given by a nursing student, is how to help someone who is choking.

▨ Task 13

Read the script aloud with your group or partner. As you read, ask yourself what strategies she uses. Also think about how she develops her introduction. Then answer the questions below.

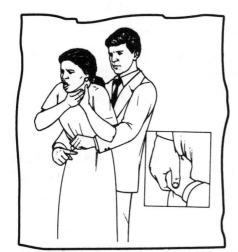

(From American Red Cross, *Adult CPR,* Copyright 1993, St. Louis, MO, Mosby Lifeline.)

How to Help Someone Who Is Choking

1. Hello everybody. If one of our classmates started choking seriously within the next few minutes, ask yourself—would you be able to help him or her? And how would you help him or her?

2. I think you know that most emergencies happen uh in or near the home, so you are more likely to give care to a family member or a friend than someone you don't know. So knowing how to rescue people from choking is worthwhile. And so today I am going to tell you how to help people who are choking.

3. Choking is a serious breathing emergency. A person who's choking has his or her airway blocked by food or another object. The airway can be partially blocked or can be completely blocked. A person who has a partially blocked airway can breathe in enough air to cough or even speak.

4. So if you see that the victim is coughing forcefully, what you should do is to encourage him or her to cough up the object. However, if a person's airway becomes completely blocked, the person can't cough forcefully, speak, or breathe. So what you must do is immediately give a series of quick hard thrusts to the victim's abdomen so that the air in the lungs will push the object out of the airway. Before I move on to the steps for giving abdominal thrusts, any questions?

5. Okay, so let's go on to the steps for giving abdominal thrusts. This is a conscious person and you can see the person is choking. *(Speaker makes choking noises)* First, you stand behind the victim and put your arms around the victim's waist. Make a fist with one hand and put the thumb side of the fist here in the victim's abdomen right above the navel but under the rib cage. That's clear?

6. And then the second step. Put your other hand on your fist and make quick, inward and upward thrusts into the abdomen, like this. *(Demonstrates while she is speaking)* And uh, you have to repeat this until the victim coughs up the object.

7. So you can do it by yourself right now. So let's practice it because I think this is helpful. Just just place your fist about the navel and below the rib cage. And then grab your fist and make an inward and upward movement. *(Demonstrates)* You can feel the pressure. Don't make it forcefully.

8. So, any questions about this procedure? Okay.

(The speaker goes on to discuss what to do if the victim is unconscious.)

(Speech by Tassanee Prasopkittikun, with slight modifications.)

Discussion Questions

1. How does the speaker open her speech?

2. What background information does she provide before explaining the steps in the process?

3. Where does the speaker begin discussing the first step?

4. What linking words does the speaker use in her speech, especially to move from one step to another?

5. What tense does the speaker use to explain the steps?

6. The speaker doesn't use passive voice to discuss the steps. What does she use instead and why?

7. What modal does the speaker use in section 6? Why?

8. What ways does the speaker keep in touch with the audience?

Examples of Cleft Sentences Using *What*

Look at the following sentences from section 4 of the speech.

- So if you see that the victim is coughing forcefully, what you should do is to encourage him or her to cough up the object.

- So what you must do is immediately give a series of quick hard thrusts to the victim's abdomen.

Notice that here the speaker used what is called a cleft sentence using *what*. The speaker may have used this construction as a means of highlighting or giving extra focus to important information that follows. A *wh*-clause begins the sentence and is generally followed by *is* or another form of *to be*. Try using a cleft sentence with *what* if you want to stress an important step in your process.

■ Task 14

If you are in an area of studies in which you give instructions to colleagues, clients, or students, give an instructions speech to the class. If possible, choose a topic that may contain useful information for a general academic audience, such as the one above on how to help someone who is choking. Follow the guidelines in task 10 on page 76. Evaluate your presentation using the evaluation sheet on pages 78–79.

■ Task 15

Give an instructions speech on an aspect of academic life. Choose a topic that will be helpful to the audience or to someone in your area of studies. For example, explain how to get into the doctoral program in your department, how to become a licensed professional in a particular field, or how to file a request for a grade review. Follow the guidelines in task 10 on page 76. Evaluate your presentation using the evaluation sheet on pages 78–79.

Defining a Concept

In this unit you will present an extended definition of a concept from your field of studies. In a sense, you have already given two extended definition speeches. When you described an object, you elaborated on the basic definition of the object by describing its physical characteristics and discussing the functions of its different parts. When you described a process, you extended the definition of the process by describing each of the steps in the process. These strategies are common in an academic setting. This unit will discuss additional ways to extend the basic definition of a concept.

Definitions are very common in academic discourse. We encounter them when we are reviewing a textbook before class or reading a research paper. We also hear them when we attend lectures and talks. In fact, it is difficult to imagine a lecture that does not contain a definition either as part of the speaker's text or in response to a question.

You may need to give an oral definition as part of

1. A class discussion

2. A discussion with your research or study group

3. A formal or informal talk

4. An oral examination or thesis defense

Defining in a general sense is simply pointing out the unique, distinguishing properties of a concept in a particular context. In an academic environment, definitions can be important when words have one meaning in "general" English but another meaning in a specialized area of study. For example, in general English *appreciation* can refer to our grateful feelings, while in business it refers to the increase in the value of land or other possessions. In addition, words may have different meanings depending on one's field of study. In dentistry, for instance, *enamel* is the hard outer covering of our teeth, while in materials science, *enamel* is an opaque coating that is baked on metal or ceramic.

Some terms can often be defined in one sentence or even a word. However, when you define an important concept in your area of studies, your goal may be to extend its basic definition by providing more specific information or details so that the listener has a richer understanding of its meaning.

▪ Task 1

How would you define *battery?* How does the speaker define it in the following speech, "Definition of a Battery"? In pairs or small groups, read the speech aloud. As you read, think about how the speaker has chosen to develop the definition. Then answer the questions that follow the speech.

Definition of a Battery

1. Okay, imagine yourself in this situation: You're going across campus to a class. Uh, you're walking with a student of the opposite sex from your department who's going to the same class. All of a sudden, this person's spouse, who turns out to be really jealous, comes up and like punches you in the nose.

2. It turns out that your nose is broken, and uh by the time you finish paying all your medical expenses, your bill adds up to over one thousand dollars. You want the spouse to pay for the damages you suffered. In this situation, *damages* is compensation for your financial loss. Okay? *(The speaker writes "damages" on the blackboard.)*

3. So you go to the student legal services office, and uh uh the lawyer there tells you that you might be able to sue the spouse for damages under a legal theory or principle called a *battery. (The speaker writes "battery" on the blackboard.)*

4. So, what's a battery? A battery is intentional touching of another person. *(The speaker begins to reveal information on her transparency.)* A battery is intentional touching of another person. *(Points to the words on the transparency)* Let me explain what I mean by intentional touching.

5. There are a lot of social situations where we intentionally touch each other, you know for example when we shake hands or tap someone on the shoulder. But, uh, a battery is intentional touching that's harmful or offensive, like hitting or punching someone.

6. In addition, to recover damages or um get compensation, the touching must cause injury. Injury is defined in two ways: physical injury and injury to someone's dignity. An example of physical injury is a head concussion. An example of an injury to someone's dignity would be um an insult to a person's race or nationality.

7. So, a battery is intentional touching. It's harmful or offensive touching, and uh it causes physical injury or injury to someone's dignity. Everybody understand so far? *(Audience answers yes)*

8. Let's focus for a minute on the term *touching*. In law, a battery also extends to uh intentional offensive touching that involves indirect contact. By *indirect* I mean contact with something that is touching you, like the books you're carrying or the clothes you're wearing. I mean, for example, suppose someone comes up and grabs the hood of your jacket and drags you to the ground, but doesn't actually touch you. That's indirect contact. Okay?

9. The definition of battery also extends to uh to what is called *causing to touch*. For instance, you come into class and begin to sit down in your desk but someone pulls the desk out from under you and and you fall on the floor. Even though the person didn't touch you, he or she caused you to touch the floor.

10. So, the definition of touching can include um indirect contact or causing a person to to touch something.

11. Okay. Now let's go back to our hypothetical broken-nose situation. Let me ask you some questions:

> Did the spouse intend to touch you? *(Audience answers yes)*
>
> And was the touching harm uh harmful or offensive? *(Audience answers yes, harmful)*
>
> By the way, um what kind of touching was it? I mean was it direct or indirect? *(Audience answers direct.)*
>
> Did you suffer injury? *(Audience answers yes, physical injury, a broken nose)*

12. Since the answer to these three questions is yes, then the spouse may have committed a battery and you may be able to receive damages to cover your medical costs.

13. So, does everyone have a general understanding of what a battery is? Yes? Any final questions?

Discussion Questions

1. How does the speaker begin the speech?

2. In what section does the speaker begin the actual definition of her speech? How does she begin it?

3. In section 4, why does the speaker repeat the definition?

4. How does the speaker extend the definition of *battery?*

5. What kind of audience is the speaker addressing—a group of law students or a more general academic audience?

6. What are some strategies that the speaker uses to maintain a relationship with the audience throughout the speech?

7. The speaker uses *okay* several times in her presentation. Look at sections 1, 2, and 11. How is *okay* used in these cases?

8. What's the purpose of *so* in sections 3, 7, and 10? Could the speaker have used *okay* instead of *so* in sections 7 and 10?

9. Look at the transparency reproduced below. How does the transparency help the speaker as well as the audience? How do you think the speaker revealed the information on the transparency?

Definition of a Battery

1. Intentional touching of another person
2. Touching is harmful or offensive
3. Touching causes injury
   Physical
   To dignity
4. Can include indirect contact
5. Can include causing to touch

___

Hypothetical Situation
Test

- Did the spouse intend to touch you?   Yes   No
- Was the touching harmful or
  offensive?   Yes   No
- Did you suffer injury?   Yes   No

In this speech, the speaker maintains a relationship with the audience by using several different strategies.

- She begins with a hypothetical story that includes the audience.
- She uses a rhetorical question to introduce the concept she is defining.
- She repeats the basic definition of *battery* in case members of the audience didn't understand it the first time.
- As she goes through each element or essential part of a battery, she uses examples to clarify what she means.
- She defines other unknown terms.
- She stops several times along the way to check if the audience is following. She also asks the audience if they have questions.
- During her speech, she summarizes what she has said so far.
- She tests the audience's understanding of *battery* by asking them questions. She asks the audience to decide if a battery has taken place.

The speaker is likely speaking to an audience with little academic legal knowledge. If she were speaking to listeners with a legal background, she might choose a different way to present the topic. In addition, her style is somewhat instructional. She treats her speech like a class lesson. This strategy helps her develop more interaction with members of the audience.

Notice that in this speech, the speaker uses *okay* in three different ways. One is to announce to the audience that the speech is going to begin (section 1). Another is to let the audience know that the speaker is going to go on to a new section of the speech (section 11). The third is to check with the audience to make sure they are following (section 8). The speaker uses *so* throughout the speech. Three common ways she uses *so* are to show result, to summarize, and to conclude.

▨ Task 2: Fillers

You may have noticed that when the speaker paused during her speech, she sometimes inserted words or parts of words that didn't add to the content of her speech. These are called *fillers*. Look at the following examples and circle the fillers that the speaker inserted.

1. Uh, you're walking with a student of the opposite sex from your department who's going to the same class.

2. All of a sudden, this person's spouse, who turns out to be really jealous, comes up and like punches you in the nose.

3. There are a lot of social situations where we intentionally touch each other, you know for example when we shake hands or tap someone on the shoulder.

4. By *indirect* I mean contact with something that was touching you, like the books you're carrying or the clothes you're wearing. I mean, for example, suppose someone comes up and grabs the hood of your jacket and drags you to the ground, but doesn't actually touch you. That's indirect contact.

5. For instance, you come into class and begin to sit down in your desk but someone pulls the desk out from under you and and you fall on the floor.

6. And was the touching harm uh harmful or offensive?

Fillers like *um* and *uh* and even repetitions like *uh uh, and and,* and *harm uh harmful* are a normal part of spoken presentations.* One reason speakers use fillers is to give themselves a space for thinking what they're going to say next. However, when you evaluate your speech, if you feel that you have too many fillers and pauses, you may need to practice more so that you sound more fluent. Fillers such as *like, you know,* and *I mean* are rather informal and also potentially confusing to the listener because they have other meanings. Even though they are used extensively in casual conversation, speakers may wish to avoid them in more formal presentations. (In number 4 above, compare the two uses of *I mean.*)

Discussion Question

1. What fillers from your own language do you find yourself using when you speak English? Could any of them potentially interfere with the audience's comprehension?

Developing or Extending a Definition

In the "Definition of a Battery" speech, the speaker introduces a brief definition of *battery* in section 4. Later in section 6, however, she gives a more complete definition. She then goes on to refine the definition even further, using examples to clarify each refinement. This is only one approach. There are many other ways to develop or extend a definition.

The following table contains an incomplete list of types of information that can be found in an extended definition. Definition speeches may contain one or more of these. Which types have you used in the speeches you have already given? Add other types as you think of them.

---

*To better understand the extent to which academic English speakers use fillers, go to the Michigan Corpus of Academic Spoken English site at <www.hti.umich.edu/m/micase/>.

Types of Information in an Extended Definition

An enumeration of the characteristics or features

A discussion of different types or kinds

A description of the structure or components

Examples

A description of how something is made

A discussion of how something works or is carried out

A description of applications

A discussion of the history or evolution of the concept, including its future potential

A comparison/contrast with a similar concept

▨ Task 3

In groups, pick several words from the list of words that follows and discuss how you would extend your definition of each of them. You can also mention other types of information not listed above.

Word	Possible ways to extend the definition
folk art	
semiconductor	
microenterprise	
oligarchy	
protein	
hurricane	
polymer	
opera	
antibiotic	
acrylic	
erosion	
pagoda	

■ Task 4: Organizing Extended Definitions

When you decide the type of information you want to include in your expanded definition, a strategy (or several strategies) for organizing the information will generally reveal itself to you. The organizational plan you choose will, in turn, suggest possible connectors or signposts you can use to create a smooth, coherent flow of speech.

Which strategy (strategies) listed would you use in organizing an extended definition with the following types of information?

Chronological order   Spatial order

Classification (organization by category)   Listing

_____ I want to talk about the characteristics or features of semiconductors.

_____ In the first part of my speech, I plan to describe the parts of a pagoda.

_____ When I define *opera,* I'd like to include a brief history of opera and the major parts of an opera.

_____ I'll focus on three common kinds of erosion and describe how each type takes place.

Opening a Definition Speech

In the "Definition of a Battery" speech, the speaker began by describing a hypothetical situation rather than beginning with "Today, I'm going to define *battery.*" In fact, she didn't introduce *battery* until section 4. One purpose of the hypothetical situation is to get the audience interested in the topic. Another is to place the word in a context. There are many effective ways to open a definition speech. However, the concept you define may be more suited to one type of opening than another. In addition, the audience and purpose of the speech may influence the type of opening you choose.

■ Task 5

Look at the following four introductions to a definition speech and discuss with a partner or group how the speakers began their presentations. Then discuss how the speakers might extend their definitions.

1. If you've gone camping before, you've probably had to take along a lot of equipment and supplies. One common camping supply that campers are

familiar with is dehydrated food. By dehydrated food, I mean food that has had most of its moisture taken out. As a result, it weighs less, which makes it ideal for camping trips. So, dehydration is the process of removing moisture from food. Dehydration also preserves food because it retards enzyme action, which makes it safer to eat. Food has been preserved for centuries by means of dehydration. Today, five modern methods are used to dehydrate food.

2. Has everybody heard of the Hollywood superstar Mel Gibson? *(Most audience members answer yes.)* Then some of you may have seen his film *Forever Young.* In this film, Mel's body is frozen in a gigantic machine. Fifty years later he thaws out and comes back to life. Well, freezing human beings is mainly done in Hollywood, but freezing human material such as blood and tissue is more common than people realize. Cryobiology is an area of science that studies the use of biological living material at extremely low temperatures.

3. What does *wife* mean? The American Heritage Dictionary defines *wife* as "a woman married to a man." However, in law, *wife* can be considered a legal term since a woman who gets married enters into a legal relationship which can alter her rights. In American law the definition of *wife* has changed over time mainly because a wife's legal rights have changed.

4.   each day an Autumn . . .
        fire and sweetness in your hearts
        apples on the stove

The type of poem I just read is called haiku. Haiku is a three-line poem containing a total of seventeen syllables, five in the first line, seven in the second, and five in the third. (Haiku by Niki Ford.)

Strategies for opening your speech

The following is a list of strategies for opening a definition speech. The speaker may decide to use more than one strategy. These strategies can also be used in other types of speeches as a means of getting the audience's attention and establishing the context. Add some strategies of your own.

1. A rhetorical question

2. A question to the audience that is meant to elicit a response

3. A hypothetical situation or short anecdote

4. An example

5. An opening statement that places the concept in a context

6. Historical background

7. A picture

8. Music or other sounds

9. A quote, a poem, or a saying

10.

11.

■ Task 6

Choose a term from your field of studies. Write an attention-getting opening for your speech that is compatible with the term you have chosen. Share it with the class. Then discuss with the class ways in which you might extend your definition.

Term:

Speech opening:

Ways to expand the definition and organizational strategy (strategies):

Formal Definitions

In academic writing, a writer frequently introduces a term to be defined with a one-sentence three-part definition.* In academic speaking, the presenter may use a three-part definition or may prefer a more informal means. The three parts of a formal definition are:

- The term

- The class in which the term belongs

- The characteristics that distinguish it from other terms in the class

---

*For a useful discussion of definitions in science lectures, see John Flowerdew, "Definitions in Science Lectures," *Applied Linguistics* 13, no. 2 (June 1992): 202–21.

▨ Task 7

Look at the following definitions and quickly underline the three parts of each definition:

(term)　　　(class)　　　(distinguishing characteristics)

1. A membrane is a thin wall that/which allows certain types of substances to pass through.

2. A battery is harmful or offensive touching that causes physical injury or injury to someone's dignity.

3. An herbicide is a chemical substance that is used to kill unwanted plants.

4. An equilateral triangle is a triangle/one which has sides of equal length.

5. Loam is a type of soil that primarily consists (soil primarily consisting) of sand, clay, silt, and other organic matter.

6. A cataract is an eye abnormality in which the lens becomes opaque, causing blindness.

7. A seismograph is a device with which an earthquake is measured.

Notice that

- The distinguishing characteristics are contained in the relative clause that begins with *that* or *which* (sentences 1–5) or a preposition plus *which* (sentences 6 and 7).

- It may also be possible to use a part of the term as the class or *one* (such as triangle/*one* in sentence 4) especially if the word is well known.

- Sometimes it is possible to use a reduced relative clause (*soil consisting* in sentence 5). How could you reduce the definition of *herbicide* in sentence 3 and the definition of *equilateral triangle* in sentence 4?

▨ Task 8: Other Ways to Define a Term

The following are examples of other ways to introduce a term in spoken academic English. Look at these definitions with a partner or group. How do they differ from the three-part formal definition presented above? Which ones seem to you to be less formal? Why?

1. What's the definition of seismoscope? It's a device you use to measure the time an earthquake occurs.

2. By seismoscope, I mean a device that measures the time an earthquake occurs.

3. A seismoscope can be defined as a device that measures the time an earthquake takes place.

4. Seismoscopes measure the time an earthquake takes place.

▨ Task 9

Now go back to the four openings of definition speeches in task 5. Find the concept(s) that each speaker introduced and defined. Which speakers used a three-part definition? What other forms did speakers choose?*

Defining Additional Terms

In the "Definition of a Battery" speech you noticed that in order to fully define *battery,* the speaker uses words that are unfamiliar to the audience. In order to be certain the audience is following her, the speaker also defines these additional, unfamiliar terms. She tries to make the definitions as short as possible so as not to interrupt the flow of the speech. These short definitions are sometimes referred to as substitutions. Four main types of substitutions are

Substitution	Meaning	Example
Synonym	One or several words that have the same or a similar meaning	A camera has an aperture or hole where the light passes through
Paraphrase	Words that clarify or explain the meaning of a term by rephrasing it	Rheumatoid arthritis is an auto-immune disease—the body's defense mechanism turns against itself. The materials are translucent—in other words, light can pass through them.
Example	Representatives of the term	Flooring can be made of hardwood—oak, cherry, maple, and so on.
Acronym	Initials or letters that stand for a longer term	Liquid crystal displays or LCDs*

*If the acronym is commonly used, such as RADAR, the speaker may begin with the initials and then explain what they stand for.

---

*Notice that in number 3, the speaker hasn't given her own formal definition of *wife* yet, only the dictionary definition.

▪ Task 10

Look at the following terms from the "Definition of a Battery" speech. What type of substitution does the speaker use to define the italicized terms?

_____ The lawyer tells you that you might be able to sue under a legal *theory* or principle called a battery.

_____ An example of *injury to someone's dignity* would be an insult to a person's race or nationality.

_____ In this situation, *damages* is compensation for financial loss.

_____ A battery also extends to intentional offensive touching that involves *indirect contact,* in other words, contact with something that was touching you, like the books you were carrying or the clothes you were wearing.

Using Transparencies with Outlines

Take a look at the visual aid that the speaker made for the "Definition of a Battery" presentation. It has no pictures but instead contains an outline of her speech. A speech outline can be beneficial to both the audience and the speaker for the following reasons:

- It helps the audience follow the speaker's chosen organizational pattern.

- It helps the speaker remember what s/he is going to say.

- If the audience doesn't totally understand or hear the speaker, key words and major points are likely to be included in the outline.

▨ Task 11

Look at the following information presented on a transparency. As his speech topic, this speaker chose to define the word polymer.

Introduction to Polymers

What is a polymer?

Characteristics of polymers

Molecular structures of polymers
- Linear
- Branched
- Network

Classifications of polymers
- Thermoplastics
- Rubbers
- Thermosets

Examples of polymers

Conclusion

Discussion Questions

1. What ways did he extend the definition of *polymer?*

2. Do you think the information on the transparency could be improved by using some pictures?

Let me (lemme)

Let me, which is pronounced *lemme* in fast speech, is commonly used in academic presentations. Notice that in the "Definition of a Battery" speech, the speaker uses Let me two times.

- Section 4: *Let me* explain what I mean by intentional touching.
- Section 11: *Let me* ask you some questions.

■ Task 12

Why does the speaker use *Let me* in the following sentences?

Let me add just one more thing.

Let me explain.

Let me backtrack here.

Let me digress.

Let me rephrase this.

Let me go on.

Let me just mention one (exception).

Let me see if I can come up with an example.

Let me write, I'm going to write the (words on the blackboard).

Let me close . . .

Let me answer your question in a minute.

Note: *Let's* cannot be used in place of *Let me* if the speaker sees herself as acting on her own. Compare *Let me think of another example* to *Let's think of another example.* In the second example, the speaker is inviting the audience to participate in the process.

All examples except the last are from MICASE 2000. Words in parentheses have been added. Also see John M. Swales and Bonnie Malczewski, "Discourse Management and New-Episode Flags in MICASE," *Corpus Linguistics in North America: Selections from the 1999 Symposium,* ed. Rita C. Simpson and John M. Swales (Ann Arbor: University of Michigan Press, 2001).

▮ Task 13

Prepare an extended-definition presentation of a concept from your field of study. Pick a term that you can explain to the members of a general audience. You should plan to talk a maximum of six to eight minutes. Refer to these guidelines for making your presentation.

1. Carefully construct your opening. Before introducing your term, develop an attention-getting opening and provide context for your audience. Ease your listeners into the term and definition.

2. Stress the concept you will define. Make sure you pronounce it properly. To guarantee the audience is following, use the term as the title of your visual aid and restate or rephrase the definition, if necessary.

3. Give a clear, well-constructed one- or two-sentence definition of your term. Choose a three-part definition or alternatives from the list on pages 98–99.

4. Develop or extend your definition. Refer to the list of types of information in an extended definition on page 94.

5. Choose a strategy for organizing the type(s) of information you plan to include in your definition. Use appropriate connectors or signposts to move from one part of your speech to another. Try using the connectors *let me okay,* and *so,* as well as *let's.*

6. Use substitutions to quickly clarify any terms in your speech that may be unclear to your audience. Review types of substitutions on page 99.

7. Keep in touch with your audience during the presentation. Use rhetorical or direct questions. At natural breaks in your presentation, ask questions to find out if your audience is following you. Also request questions from the audience. Include the audience as participants in your presentation, when possible.

8. Use a transparency to enhance your presentation. It can be advantageous to include your speech outline on your transparency. If you think a picture is preferable, choose one that is large and clear with bold lettering (see unit 2). Or use both an outline and a picture.

9. Practice your speech at least five or six times. Tape-record yourself twice and evaluate your progress. Listen for fillers, hesitations, and pauses. Do they sound natural, or do you need more practice? Prepare a note card, if necessary, but don't read or memorize your speech word for word.

Should you write out your speech?

Some speakers find it helpful to write out their speeches. If you are having trouble organizing material or feel somewhat unsure of how to develop your speech, writing it out with a word processor can be useful. Once you've written it, you can read through it, get a feel for how well it's developed, and make necessary changes. In addition, your instructor can look it over and offer comments before you actually make your presentation. Remember, however, to write your speech as you would say it, not read it. And don't be tempted to memorize your speech word for word once you have written it out. Trying to memorize your speech may cause you to become anxious if you forget the exact words you were going to say. Instead, make an outline visual aid that includes the main points in your speech. Eventually you may find that writing out the first few sentences of your speech and developing a good outline is more helpful than writing out your entire speech.

Interrupting the Speaker

By encouraging audience members to ask questions or ask for clarification, speakers are giving them a role in the presentation. Listeners can get the speaker's attention by raising their hand, especially during a larger or more formal presentation. If the audience is small and the situation informal, listeners who wish to ask for clarification may sometimes be able to simply interrupt the speaker. Some verbal expressions that accompany either type of interruption in an academic setting include

1. Excuse me. I'm not following this. . . (Asks a question.)

2. I wonder if you could say a bit (more about) . . .

3. I was wondering if you'd . . .

4. Could you repeat that question?

5. Can you repeat? I didn't get the (definition).

6. I'm sorry. A *what* topic?

7. I didn't catch that.

8. I'm just a bit confused.

All examples are from MICASE 2000. Words in parentheses have been added.

- In which example is the listener asking the speaker to repeat only one or two words?

- What does the expression "I didn't get . . ." in example 5 mean?

Notice the strategies that speakers use to soften requests *(I wonder, I was wondering if you'd, Could you)*. None of the strategies includes *please*. This may be because *please* tends to be used with more direct or even more demanding requests in English and has the potential for being less polite, as in *Please repeat that.**

---

*See Susan M. Reinhart and Ira Fisher, "Offers of Help and Requests for Help," in *Speaking and Social Interaction* (Ann Arbor: University of Michigan Press, 2000).

Prespeech Evaluation

Definition Speech Evaluation Form

Name: _____

Question	(Make a check in the appropriate column)			Comments
	Yes	Maybe	No	
Did you use an attention-getting opener?				
Did you place the concept in a context before defining it?				
Did you give a well-constructed one-sentence definition of the term?				
Did you pronounce the term correctly?				
Did you say the definition slowly and clearly, emphasizing the key words in the sentence and repeating or rephrasing where necessary?				
Did you extend the definition in a way or ways that made your speech interesting?				
Did you carefully organize information? Explain.				
Did you define other terms as you gave your speech using substitutions, such as synonyms, paraphrases, examples, and acronyms?				
Did you stay in touch with the audience? If so, how?				
Was your visual aid clear and easy to read?				
Was the term included in the title of your visual aid?				

Question	(Make a check in the appropriate column)			Comments
	Yes	Maybe	No	
Did you display an outline or use some other means of guiding the audience through the presentation?				
Did you use *Let me* to tell the audience what you were going to do next?				
Did you practice enough so that your speech wasn't hesitant and choppy and you didn't overuse fillers?				

Pronunciation
(specific comments)

Other comments

Goals for your next presentation (list 2–3 areas that you want to improve on for your next presentation)

Final Evaluation

Definition Speech Evaluation Form				

Name: _____

Question	(Make a check in the appropriate column)			Comments
	Yes	Maybe	No	
Did you use an attention-getting opener?				
Did you place the concept in a context before defining it?				
Did you give a well-constructed one-sentence definition of the term?				
Did you pronounce the term correctly?				
Did you say the definition slowly and clearly, emphasizing the key words in the sentence and repeating or rephrasing where necessary?				
Did you extend the definition in a way or ways that made your speech interesting?				
Did you carefully organize information? Explain.				
Did you define other terms as you gave your speech using substitutions, such as synonyms, paraphrases, examples, and acronyms?				
Did you stay in touch with the audience? If so, how?				
Was your visual aid clear and easy to read?				
Was the term included in the title of your visual aid?				

Question	(Make a check in the appropriate column)			Comments
	Yes	Maybe	No	
Did you display an outline or use some other means of guiding the audience through the presentation?				
Did you use *Let me* to tell the audience what you were going to do next?				
Did you practice enough so that your speech wasn't hesitant and choppy and you didn't overuse fillers?				

Pronunciation
(specific comments)

Other comments

Goals for your next presentation (list 2–3 areas that you want to improve on for your next presentation)

Unit 4 Supplementary Materials

Pronunciation: Intonation and Noun Phrases

Unit 3 discusses intonation and how speakers use rising intonation to highlight words in English. One problem that faces nonnative speakers of English is choosing the correct intonation pattern when highlighting certain noun phrases.

Look at the following pairs of noun phrases. What is the difference between the first and the second noun phrase in each pair?

1. telephone equipment   modern equipment
2. a gum disease   a fatal disease
3. health care   adequate care
4. a system failure   a major failure
5. his career interests   his current interests
6. an engineering study   a new study

In the first noun phrase of each pair, the noun phrase is composed of two nouns, the first functioning as an adjective:

adjective (noun) + noun

Consider gerunds, such as *engineering, teaching, swimming, housing,* as nouns.

In the second noun phrase of each pair, the noun phrase consists of an adjective and a noun:

adjective + noun

In English, both the adjective and the noun are generally stressed because they provide the listener with important information. However, when nonnative speakers want to highlight the noun phrase, they find it difficult to decide on which of the two words they should use rising intonation.

Here are some general guidelines for intonation with noun phrases in English. When the noun phrase consists of an adjective (noun) + noun combination, rising intonation generally occurs on the stressed syllable of the adjective (noun).

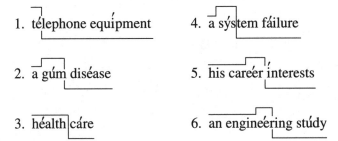

1. télephone equípment
2. a gúm diséase
3. héalth cáre
4. a sýstem fáilure
5. his careér interests
6. an engineéring stúdy

In these examples, the speaker highlights the type or category of equipment, disease, care, etc.

In contrast, when the noun phrase consists of an adjective + noun combination, rising intonation generally occurs on the stressed syllable of the noun. In these examples, the speaker highlights the noun (*equipment, disease, care,* etc.), not the adjective that describes it.

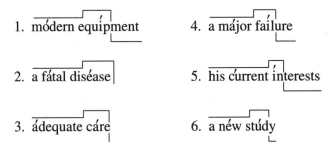

1. módern equípment
2. a fátal diséase
3. ádequate cáre
4. a májor faílure
5. his cúrrent interests
6. a néw stúdy

In all the examples above, notice that the intonation rises to high level, and then drops to low level, if the speaker comes to a full stop. If the speaker merely pauses slightly, intonation drops to mid level and the speaker continues. (Refer to the discussion in unit 3 on pp. 82–83)

In 1999, he began work as a résearch assistant. ////

First, he worked as a résearch assistant, //

and then he became a prógram óperator. ////

Guidelines for determining which word to highlight in the noun phrase are help-ful but do not apply in every case. Compare *computer skills* and *analytical skills.* *Computer* is an adjective (noun) while *analytical* is an adjective, but they are gen-erally pronounced with the same intonation pattern.

This position requires compúter skílls.

This position requires analýtical skílls.

Here the focus appears to be on the types or category of skills required. Compare, on the other hand, *computer processing* and *film processing.* Even though *com-puter* is an adjective (noun), the focus is on *processing* (cf. other types of com-puter work such as computer *programming*), not *computer.* In the second, the fo-cus is on the type of processing—*film* processing (cf. other types of processing such as *paper* processing).

Said has taught classes in compúter prócessing.

Today I'd like to continue my discussion on fílm prócessing.

When additional adjectives are added to either of the two patterns, the intonation pattern does not generally change. However, these adjectives tend to convey im-portant information and thus may also be stressed. Compare the following:

He's a résearch assístant. ////   He is a qúalified résearch assístant. ////

He's a high-lével assístant. ////   He is a qúalified high-lével assístant. ////

It is important to note that, no matter what the general guidelines are, rising into-nation can occur on any word that the speaker chooses to highlight (see unit 3, p. 83). In the following example,

That's right. This is the ólder equípment.

the speaker is reassuring the listener that she correctly understands which is the older equipment (compared to the newer equipment).

In the next example,

I said film prócessing.

a listener appears not to have heard the final word in the sentence *(processing),* and the speaker appears to be clarifying.

Task 14

In pairs or groups, practice saying the following sentences from topics discussed in this unit. Each sentence contains one or more adjective (noun) or adjective + noun combinations. You may wish to mark the intonation pattern first. See the notes to the sentences before doing this.

1. You want damages for your medical expenses.* Damages is compensation for your financial loss.

2. One type of injury is physical injury.** An example of a physical injury is a head concussion.

3. Let's go back to the broken-nose situation.

4. When you go on long hiking trips, it's important to take along enough camping supplies. One common supply campers are familiar with is dehydrated food.

5. A herbicide is a chemical substance used to kill unwanted plants.

---

*In this example, the intonation rises on *medical* in the first sentence. This is likely because the speaker wishes to emphasize the type of expenses.
**In this example, the intonation rises on *physical* in the first sentence. Here the speaker may wish to emphasize the type of injury. In the second sentence, the speaker may continue to highlight *physical* or possibly switch the emphasis to *injury.*

▨ Task 15

Before making your next presentation, write down two or three sentences from your speech that highlight adjective (noun) + noun combinations. Practice saying them using rising (high-level) intonation on the stressed syllable of the adjective (noun) followed by falling (mid-level or low-level) intonation on the noun. Check with your instructor for possible exceptions to the general guidelines.

Next, write down two or three sentences that highlight adjective + noun combinations. Practice saying them using rising (high-level) intonation on the stressed syllable of the noun followed by falling (mid-level or low-level) intonation. Check with your instructor for possible exceptions to the general guidelines.

▨ Task 16

Listen to part of one of your recorded speeches. Listen especially to sentences in which you have highlighted adjective (noun) + noun and adjective + noun combinations. Write them down and indicate the following:

- Where your intonation rises
- Where it falls
- How far it falls

What corrections would you make?

Gestures

As discussed in unit 1, novice speakers may (1) fail to use hand gestures or (2) use distracting hand movements during their speeches. Which of the following have you observed yourself doing in your first several presentations?

___ Grasping your hands behind your back

___ Grasping your hands in front of you

___ Keeping your hands in your pockets

___ Holding something in your hand that kept you from gesturing

___ Keeping your hands at your sides

___ Taking your hands in and out of your pocket

___ Making other hand movements that distracted from your speech, such as scratching your arm or touching your hair

___ Repeating the same gesture over and over

___ _____

___ _____

Have your hand gestures changed? If so, how?

How would you like to improve your gestures?

Improving Hand Gestures

Watching your own and other speakers' presentations can give you some ideas for improving your hand gestures. Here are several ways that speakers may use gestures effectively. Can you think of more?

1. Mimicking or demonstrating an action, such as pouring liquid or scraping the surface of an object.

2. Describing the object or part of the object that you are talking about, such as outlining its shape. Demonstrating a property of an object, such as showing that an object bends easily.

3. Using your hand or fingers to point, for example, to a person, a step in a process shown on a transparency, or the right-hand corner of an imaginary piece of paper.

4. Using your fingers to count.*

5. Using rhythmic, beatlike gestures to emphasize key information.

▤ Task 17

Look at the following sentences. In groups, demonstrate how you would use your hands if you were saying the sentences during a speech. Share your gestures with other groups and also ask your instructor to demonstrate the gestures s/he might use. Discuss some of the cultural differences and similarities you observed.

1. Today I'd like to introduce you to Said Al-Salem.

2. Claudine first majored in art but later switched to architecture.

3. Pong studied in Britain twice—in 1993 and again in 1997.

4. A camera has an aperture or hole where light passes through.

5. I'll answer that question in just a minute.

6. Let me write the word on the blackboard.

7. First, make a fist with your hand.

8. I'm going to describe a receipt from top to bottom.

---

*In English, what finger do speakers begin counting with?

9. So what's a battery?

10. The person's spouse comes up and punches you in the nose.

11. Injury can be defined in two ways: physical injury and injury to someone's dignity.

12. Does someone have a question? If not, let's go on to the next step.

13. This step in the process is very, very dangerous because it must be done quickly.

14. (Rankine cycle) In the condenser, the vapor is condensed to a liquid again. This cycle can be repeated again and again.

15. The process has become simpler, cheaper, and safer.

▓ Task 18

If you videotaped your last speech, look at it with the volume turned down. Watch your hands. What do you do with them? In what ways do your gestures make your speech more effective? What improvements can you make?

▓ Task 19

Choose two good speakers, such as a professor and a colleague, and observe their gestures. How do they effectively use their hands? Or watch part of a video of a university lecture. How does the speaker use gestures to enhance his or her delivery? What differences do you notice in the way good speakers use gestures in your own country?

Giving a Problem-Solution Speech

In academic environments, it is common to discuss problems and solutions. Civil engineering students talk about problems with building sites, urban planners present solutions to problems created by urban sprawl, art majors discuss ways to avoid toxic paints and art supplies, and computer scientists share ideas for overcoming limitations in current computer hardware. In this unit, you will give a problem-solution speech about a problem in your field of studies.

When giving a problem-solution speech, speakers often organize information according to this four-part structure.*

Description of a **situation**	**Situation**
Identification and description of a **problem**	**Problem**
Discussion of one or more **solutions** or **responses** to the problem	**Solution**
Evaluation of the solution(s)	**Evaluation**

In the **situation** section, the speaker provides the necessary background information for understanding the problem and how it has arisen. In the **problem** section, the speaker identifies and discusses the problem. As part of the discussion, the speaker generally explains the reasons for the problem. S/he may also discuss inadequate solutions to the problem. Depending on the nature of the problem, speakers may choose to combine the situation and problem sections. In the **solution** or **response** section, the speaker generally highlights one solution and discusses it in detail. In the **evaluation** section, the speaker evaluates the solution by pointing out its strengths and weaknesses. The last two sections may overlap, depending on how the speaker organizes information.

Two reasons to use a problem-solution pattern of organization are

1. When you are preparing your speech, this four-part structure provides you with a simple means of ordering and remembering information.

2. This familiar pattern of organization helps your audience follow your talk because they will be able to predict how your presentation will develop.**

---

*See M. Hoey, *On the Surface of Discourse* (London: Allen and Unwin, 1983).
**See R. Boyle, "Modelling Oral Presentations," *ELT Journal* 50, no. 2 (April 1996).

Some of the speech topics you have already presented can be adapted to conform to a problem-solution structure. For example, a term you have defined, such as the greenhouse effect or attention deficit disorder (ADD), might, by its nature, be considered a problem to be solved. A recently designed object or procedure may, on the other hand, be considered a solution to a problem.

◾ Task 1

In pairs or small groups, read aloud the following problem-solution speech about a plant called purple loosestrife. First, identify the different parts (situation, problem, solution, evaluation). Then, answer the questions that follow the speech.

Purple Loosestrife

(1) You may have seen a tall, bright purple plant growing along some of the rivers and lakes in this area of the United States. (2) This attractive plant is called purple loosestrife. (3) Purple loosestrife is a wetland species from Europe and Asia that was brought to the United States in the 1800s. (4) It spread naturally near water but was also spread by gardeners who noticed how beautiful it was and put it in the wet areas of their yards and gardens. (5) Now purple loosestrife covers some four hundred thousand acres in the United States and Canada. (6) Unfortunately, its extensive spread has had a serious impact on public wetlands in the U.S. (7) Why has it had such a devastating effect on these areas? (8) First, loosestrife multiplies quickly. (9) One reason is that it reproduces rapidly—one adult plant can disperse two million seeds annually. (10) Another is that it's an invasive species. (11) It doesn't have any natural enemies in the U.S. (12) As a result, it forces out native vegetation that provides food for many wetland wildlife species. (13) Second, the loosestrife plant is made up of very dense strands. (14) Because it is so thick and dense, it can't be used as cover or nesting sites for a wide range of native wetland animals, including ducks, geese, frogs, toads, and turtles. (15) And third, loosestrife seems almost indestructible. (16) The following typical plant control methods have been tried with little

success. (17) Burning. Burning doesn't control plant roots, seeds, or seedling plants. (18) Mowing. Mowing doesn't prevent seed production and can even lead to uncontrolled growth because the plant can resprout from roots and broken stems that fall to the ground or into the water. (19) And herbicides. Herbicides are expensive, and in some cases, they can make a wetland site better for loosestrife by killing off native vegetation. (20) To protect the wetlands, the U.S. Fish and Wildlife Service is now looking to natural biological controls for help. (21) One clever way to control purple loosestrife that seems to be safe and effective is to use an insect called a flower-feeding weevil. (22) Flower-feeding weevils are a species of beetle native to parts of Europe and Asia. (23) They are currently being introduced into areas of the United States where loosestrife causes the greatest problems. (24) The beetles feed on various parts of the loosestrife plant, most importantly its ovaries. This prevents the flower from reproducing. (25) These weevils have three main advantages over conventional means of controlling loosestrife. (26) First, they normally feed only on loosestrife, not on other plants. (27) Moreover, if they become established in their new environment, they should provide year-round control of the plant without any further human intervention. (28) Finally, the weevils are inexpensive. (29) At this point, the long-term success of this method in the United States isn't precisely known. (30) But the Fish and Wildlife Service is hopeful that the weevils will eat enough of the weed to control the growth of loosestrife and stop it from spreading.

Discussion Questions

1. How does the speaker raise interest in the topic?

2. What material does the speaker cover in the problem section of the speech? Why does the speaker spend so much time on this section?

3. What word(s) does the speaker use to announce the beginning of the problem section? The solution section?

4. The speaker uses the word *clever* to introduce the new solution. In trying to convince you of the reasonableness of the solution, which of the following adjectives could the speaker have effectively used instead? Why?

   adequate, innovative, convenient, interesting, proposed, tricky, neat, risky, creative

5. In her discussion of the three main advantages of her solution, what important issues does the speaker address?

6. How might the speaker have expanded the evaluation section?

The speaker uses a typical problem-solution structure for her speech. She involves the listeners in her opening statement and provides them with background information about loosestrife. She then introduces the problem of loosestrife's prolific spread and explains the reasons for the problem. In her problem section, she emphasizes the difficulty of getting rid of loosestrife by enumerating solutions that have failed to control the spread of loosestrife. By eliminating these as possible solutions, she makes it more likely that audience will be receptive to her solution.

Then, the speaker moves on to the solution section. Here she introduces a *clever* solution. Her use of *clever* informs the audience of her opinion of the solution. She could have used other adjectives, such as *creative, innovative,* or *neat* to convey basically the same meaning as *clever.* However, adjectives like *adequate, convenient, proposed, tricky, risky,* and possibly even *interesting* would not convey the speaker's enthusiasm for the solution to the audience. In her evaluation section, the speaker addresses important issues of harm to the environment, the need for human intervention, and cost. She acknowledges that there is no long-term data on the benefits of the flower-feeding weevils. However, she might have been able to present some evidence of the beetle's short-term positive effects in places where it has been introduced or a foreseeable limitation of this method.

Strategies to Signal Problems or Disadvantages

In a problem-solution speech, the speaker generally informs the audience that s/he is moving from the situation to the problem by means of a linking word or other signal that announces the problem. Here are three common strategies that speakers use to introduce a problem.

Adversative signposts that signal that a situation has created a problem	*but, however, although, even though, nevertheless, in spite of* + noun
Adverbs that introduce a problem	*unfortunately, sadly*
Phrases that indicate a problem	*The problem is that . . .* *This need for land has caused (led to) a serious problem.* *An unfortunate result of this decision is that . . .*

These strategies may be effectively combined, as in *Unfortunately, this has caused a serious problem* or *The problem, however, is that . . .*

- In what other part of a problem-solution speech can these same strategies be used?

Strategies to Signal a Solution

In a problem-solution speech, the speaker moves from the problem to the solution by using a signal that announces the solution. The following are four common ways to introduce a solution in English. Notice that all of them contain an infinitive (*to* + verb).

	Example
A purpose statement using the infinitive (In order) to + verb	*(In order) to reduce the spread of loosestrife,* scientists have introduced beetles that eat the weed.
The expression *One way* + to solve the problem is to + verb	*One way to control purple loosestrife that seems safe and effective is to* use beetles that eat the weed.
The expression *One solution to the problem is to* + verb (or verb + *ing*)	*One solution to the uncontrolled spread of loosestrife* is to introduce natural biological controls.

Listing

In the "Purple Loosestrife" speech, the speaker makes abundant use of listing strategies to organize information: (1) She lists three reasons that loosestrife has had a serious effect on public wetlands. (2) She lists two reasons that loosestrife multiplies quickly. (3) She lists three unsuccessful solutions to the problem. (4) In her solution section, she lists three advantages of the solution she advocates. Listing is a simple and frequently used organizational tool in academic speaking.

- What listing connectors does the speaker use in these three places? Circle them.

An array of information can be organized in this way, such as reasons for a procedure, disadvantages of a method, proposed solutions, and the main parts of an object. Listing can be easily incorporated into a broader organizational pattern, such as problem solution. The following are common listing connectors in English.

- Enumerators—ordinal numbers*
  first
  second
  third

- Other listing connectors or additives,** such as
  furthermore
  in addition
  moreover
  what's more
  also
  plus
  besides
  finally
  and last
  one clever solution is . . . another is . . .
  the most dangerous problem is . . . others include . . .

---

*Notice that *at first* isn't in this list. *First* is used as an enumerator but not *at first*. *At first* is used when the speaker originally introduces one idea, belief, method, plan, and so forth, and then changes it. For example: *At first, it seemed loosestrife was harmless, but then environmentalists noticed it was pushing out native plants.*

**Notice that *at last* isn't on this list. *Finally* and *last* can be used as additives, but *at last* cannot. *At last* means "after a long time." For example: *At last, scientists have found a way to control loosestrife.*

- Noun phrases, gerunds, imperatives, or other expressions that summarize the elements or items in the list. For example:

  Burning. Burning doesn't control plant roots, seeds, or seedling plants.
  Mowing. Mowing doesn't prevent seed production.

In this method, the speaker effectively highlights the topic of the sentence before saying the whole sentence.

- A bullet strategy using cardinal numbers.

  This solution has the following advantages:

  One, it's inexpensive.
  Two, it's readily available.
  And three, it's been proven effective against the spread of loosestrife.

  This method is fast-paced and effective for presenting short lists.

- A bullet strategy with no listing connectors

  This solution has the following advantages:

  It's inexpensive.
  It's readily available.
  It's effective.

In this strategy, the speaker simply presents the contents of the list without using enumerators or other listing strategies. This method is quick-paced and direct, and can be effective when presenting short lists.

Speaking to Persuade: Providing Evidence

In academic speaking, one of our goals as presenters may be to persuade listeners to our position on a given topic. Much persuasive academic discourse centers around problems and solutions. For example, business and economics students may be expected to convince the audience that there is an impending financial crisis. In other words, they must persuade the audience that there is a problem. Educators may be asked to justify their curriculum design, or psychologists to defend their choice of one treatment plan over others. In other words, they may be expected to defend their solution to a perceived problem.

Our ability to persuade depends in part on the supporting evidence we provide. However, members of different academic communities don't necessarily attempt to persuade their audiences in the same way. In some fields, stories and other anecdotal evidence may be convincing, while in others statistical data may be highly regarded. Persuasive evidence is generally defined by the members of a particular discipline. Even then, not everyone in that discipline may agree.

▨ Task 2

Different types of evidence may be needed at different stages of the problem-solution speech. In your area of studies, what types of evidence are generally used to show that there is a problem? What types of evidence would be used to evaluate a particular solution? Refer to the list that follows and put a check in the appropriate column(s).

To Indicate a Problem	To Evaluate a Solution	Evidence
		1. Results of research studies/tests
		2. Questionnaires, surveys, and other collected data
		3. General knowledge, facts
		4. Observations, observations over time
		5. Description of symptoms, feelings
		6. Anecdotal or experiential evidence
		7. Physical evidence or pictures
		8. Other (write in type):
		9. Other (write in type):

▨ Task 3

Look at the following problem-solution speech from another academic area, medicine. Using the list above, check the types of evidence that the speaker uses in his presentation. Then answer the questions that follow.

Thyroid Hormone Replacement

(Introduction and speech overview have been omitted.)

(1) The thyroid is a gland located at the base of the front of the neck. (2) It's an important part of the endocrine system because it helps control bodily functions like metabolism and mental development. (3) One common

medical condition that involves the thyroid is called *hypothyroidism,* which basically means that the thyroid gland doesn't produce enough or any thyroid hormone. (4) This can cause a number of symptoms such as depression, muscle and joint pain, fatigue, intolerance of cold temperatures, weight gain, and decreased memory. (5) The problem is usually easy to treat. (6) Patients are given synthetic thyroid called thyroxine (levothyroxine), or T4. (7) If the right dose is prescribed, it's considered safe, and symptoms start to disappear soon after a patient starts taking T4. (8) However, a small percentage of patients report that they continue to suffer from at least some of the symptoms of hypothyroid even though their blood tests show that their hormone levels have returned to normal. (9) Some doctors have begun to attribute this in part to the fact that patients only take T4, even though the thyroid gland also produces another hormone, triiodothyronine (liothyronine) or T3. (10) In the past it was thought that T4 converted to T3 in the body, so it wasn't necessary to prescribe T3. (11) However, there's anecdotal evidence by patients that they have fewer symptoms if they take T3 along with T4. (12) A recent study done in Lithuania that was reported in the *New England Journal of Medicine* seems to support these patients' observations. (13) Patients felt better if they took both hormones. (14) In the study, which involved some 30 patients, the subjects who took both T4 and T3 reported less depression and better concentration than the ones taking T4 alone. (15) The study concluded that T3 "improved the quality of life for most patients."

(16) Nevertheless, most doctors are reluctant to try the T4/T3 combination. (17) First, they say that T4 has been successful for most patients and they feel that there's not enough evidence to convince them to use T3 at this time. (18) They also worry that because T3 is quickly absorbed by the body, it can increase heart rate. (19) The Lithuania study showed that the heart rate of participants taking T3 did increase slightly but not significantly. (20) And while doctors who have promoted the use of T3 agree that it can increase the

heart rate, they also say this problem can be solved by prescribing time-release capsules. (21) Doctors who are skeptical of T3 also say that there is not enough information available on the optimum combination of T3 and T4. (22) But the problem seems to be caused in part by their own refusal to prescribe T3. (23) Those doctors who prescribe T3 are generally willing to work with patients to find the right dose combination. (24) A more practical problem for patients is that at this time T3 isn't usually available in pharmacies. (25) Prescriptions for T3 must be specially compounded by a pharmacist and may not be covered by insurance. (27) This obstacle may be removed in the future if further research confirms that at least some of the problems that patients continue to have can be solved by T3.

Discussion Questions

1. What kind of evidence does the speaker offer to show that there is a problem?

2. What types of evidence does the speaker provide as support for the solution?

3. How has the speaker designed the evaluation section?

4. Do you think that the speaker successfully responds to criticism of the solution?

5. In his solution section, the speaker summarizes a study from the *New England Journal of Medicine*. What additional information would you like the speaker to provide about the study or what questions or criticism might you have about the study?

While the speaker provides anecdotal evidence from patients to show there is a problem, he doesn't wholly rely on anecdotal evidence to support his solution. He also discusses the results of a recently published research study. In his evaluation section, the speaker informs the audience of additional criticisms doctors have had of the solution and addresses these criticisms. In fact, he himself poses a practical disadvantage of the solution. The speaker doesn't give specific details about the study, perhaps because he is talking to a general academic audience. An astute audience might request more details about the subjects, how the study was carried out, how long the study lasted, etc.

Revealing Disadvantages to Your Solution

To protect yourself from criticism, you may find it useful to acknowledge the benefits of other solutions even while highlighting their limitations. You should also be prepared to make a critical appraisal of your own solution and to respond to the counterarguments of your opponents. Since your critics will be quick to point out weaknesses in your solution, you may find yourself in a stronger position if you bring them up first. You can minimize the disadvantages of your solution by pointing out that the disadvantages

1. Are minor or easily overcome

2. Are less serious than disadvantages of other solutions

3. Will likely be reduced over time

Which of these strategies did the "Thyroid Hormone Replacement" speaker use?

Disadvantages	Response
T4 has been successful with most patients, not enough evidence on T3 to convince them to use it	Future research
T3 increases the heart rate	Not significantly; possible to take time capsules
Not enough information on the optimum combination of T3 and T4	Problem caused in part by their refusal to work with patients to find the right combination
Prescriptions not readily available; may not be covered by insurance	Further research may remove this obstacle

Hedging: Qualifying Your Claims

Another way that you can protect yourself from criticism from the audience is by using hedging strategies. Hedging strategies are ways you can soften your position by qualifying or limiting your claims.

Task 4

Look at the following statements from the "Purple Loosestrife" speech. Does the speaker use a hedging strategy? Explain.

1. Burning. Burning doesn't control plant roots, seeds, or seedling plants.

2. (Weevils) normally feed only on loosestrife, not on other plants.

3. (Weevils) should provide year-round control of the plant without any further human intervention.

4. (The) Fish and Wildlife Service is hopeful that the weevils will eat enough of the weed to control the growth of loosestrife and stop it from spreading.

Task 5

Look at statements from the "Thyroid Hormone Replacement" speech. Does the speaker use a hedging strategy? Explain. Where the speaker has weakened his claim, how could he strengthen it?

1. A recent study in the *New England Journal of Medicine* seems to support these patients' observations.

2. The study concluded that T3 "improved the quality of life for most patients."

3. This obstacle may be removed in the future if further research confirms that at least some of the problems that patients continue to have can be solved by T3.

4. Doctors who are skeptical of T3 also say that there is not enough information available on the optimum combination of T3 and T4. But the problem seems to be caused in part by their own refusal to prescribe T3.

There are many ways to hedge in English, including using modals *(may, should)*, adverbs *(normally, sometimes, rarely, likely)*, adjectives *(some, most)*, conditionals *(if)*, and prepositional phrases *(in the short term, under these circumstance, for a small number of people, in this geographical area, men under the age of 50)*.

Concluding Your Speech

Many speakers who carefully plan and practice their speeches still find themselves at a loss at the end of their presentation because they are unsure how to conclude their speeches. They may end their speeches abruptly (e.g., *that's all*) or may drag out their speech by making several attempts to conclude.

■ Task 6

Look at the following speech endings. In pairs or small groups, discuss the strategies that the speakers have used to conclude their speeches. Check the ones you think are the most effective. Put a 0 in front of those you think are the least effective. Be prepared to explain your choices.

___ 1. So, that's all I have to say about polymers.

___ 2. That's the end of my speech on polymers. Thanks for listening. I know it was hard to understand.

___ 3. Today I've defined the term *polymer.* I've discussed the characteristics of polymers and have explained the different types of polymers. I've also given you examples of polymers. Do you have any questions?

___ 4. Now I think you're able to understand why the characteristics of polymers lend themselves to creating many of the products that we use in our homes today. Any final questions?

___ 5. In summary, the harp is a unique instrument. You can see how different it is. None of the other musical instruments are like the harp. Thank you.

___ 6. In conclusion, today I've described the major parts of the harp and their functions. Thank you.

___ 7. So that's a simple description of the major parts of the harp and their functions. What you haven't been able to hear today is the beautiful sound the harp makes. Hopefully, you'll have the chance to hear the harp being played at one of the Music School's concerts this semester. Any questions?

___ 8. So today I've discussed the major parts of a deciduous tree and their functions. Next time I'll discuss the process by which deciduous trees lose their leaves each year. Any final questions?

____ 9. It is important that we check the spread of loosestrife. If we don't, the plant will continue to expand and harm wetlands all across the nation. Any comments or questions?

____ 10. At this point, the long-term success of this method in the United States isn't precisely known. But the Fish and Wildlife Service is hopeful that the weevils will eat enough of the weed to control its growth and stop it from spreading.

____ 11. So, even though the results aren't in yet, it looks like the flower-feeding weevil is a promising solution to the serious problem of un-controlled growth of loosestrife. So far we know that they help stop loosestrife from reproducing, shouldn't harm other plants, and are in-expensive. Over the next few years, we should be able to observe its effectiveness in the United States.

What signpost did the presenter use to signal to the audience that she was about to end her "Battery" speech on page 90? ("So, does everyone have a general understanding of what a battery is? Yes? Any final questions?")

What signposts were used in the endings above to indicate that the speaker was about to conclude?

Tips on Concluding Your Presentation

When you design a conclusion for your speech, you may wish to ask yourself the following questions:

1. What do you want the purpose of your conclusion to be? For example, do you want to

    • re-emphasize the far-ranging impact or the elegance of your solution?

    • stress the importance of your topic in the listeners' daily lives?

    • leave the audience with a question to think about?

    • tie your conclusion to a question you asked or a statement you made at the beginning of your speech?

    • end with a recommendation, a hope for the future, an admonition, a plea, etc?

    • briefly mention something that you weren't able to include in your presentation and that you hope to discuss in a future presentation?

    • end with a humorous statement related to your topic?

2. Do you think it is necessary to repeat information from your speech in your conclusion? Why? Will this repetition detract from your speech?

3. How long do you think your conclusion should be? Does it need to be more than two or three sentences?

Providing an Overview or Outline Summary

After designing the first draft of her "Purple Loosestrife" speech, the speaker decides to make a change in the situation section of the speech. She adds an overview or outline summary.

Task 7

Read the change the speaker has made, sentences 7–11 (which take the place of sentences 7–8 in the speech as presented on p. 120), and answer the questions that follow the sentences. (Sentences 1–6 have been repeated.)

(1) You may have seen a tall, bright purple plant growing along some of the rivers and lakes in this area of the United States. (2) This attractive plant is called purple loosestrife. (3) Purple loosestrife is a wetland species from Europe and Asia that was brought to the United States in the 1800s. (4) It spread naturally near water but was also spread by gardeners who noticed how beautiful it was and put it in the wet areas of their yards and gardens. (5) Now purple loosestrife covers some four hundred thousand acres in the United States and Canada. (6) Unfortunately, its extensive spread has had a serious impact on public wetlands in the U.S.

(7) Today I'm going to explain why purple loosestrife has become a problem and what is being done to solve the problem. (8) First I'll discuss the reasons that loosestrife has had a serious impact on public wetlands in the United States. (9) Then I'll outline some of the methods that have been unsuccessfully used to control loosestrife. (10) And finally, I'll introduce a unique way to control loosestrife that appears to be both safe and effective. (11) All right, let's take a look at why loosestrife has had such a devastating effect on these areas. (12) First, loosestrife multiplies quickly.

Discussion Questions

1. Where does the speaker insert the overview or outline summary? What is its purpose?

2. The speaker begins the overview at sentence 7 with a one-sentence summary of her speech. Then what does she do?

3. What type of connectors does the speaker use in her overview?

4. What tense/modal does she use?

5. How does the speaker "get back" to her speech? In other words, after she finishes her overview, how does she make the transition to the problem section?

6. In the overview, does the speaker tell the audience what solution she is going to present? Why or why not?

An overview or outline summary provides a brief outline of the speech to the audience. In a typical overview, the speaker tells the audience what information to listen for and how it will be organized but doesn't generally give the audience specific content information. An overview often contains a one-sentence statement summarizing the speech topic and then a brief summary of each section of the speech. Speakers use time connectors, such as *first, then, after that,* and *finally* to indicate the order in which they will proceed. They also typically use *I'm going to* or the modal *will (I'll)* in each section of the overview. Some reasons speakers may provide an overview are the following:

1. Their speech is long.
2. Their audience is unfamiliar with the topic.
3. They want to acquaint the audience with their organizational strategy.

In order not to confuse the audience, speakers who use an overview generally don't stray or deviate from it during their speech.*

---

*If speakers sometimes find themselves digressing from their planned speech, it is helpful if they announce the digression (e.g., *Let me digress for a minute*).

Making a Transparency
to Accompany an Overview

In addition to including the overview in her presentation, the speaker has modified her transparency by adding the section in bold lettering. This section contains an outline of her overview. This way she can reveal the overview outline to the audience without revealing the outline of her speech.

Purple Loosestrife

1. **Reasons why purple loosetrife has had a serious impact on public wetlands in the U.S.**

2. **Methods that have been unsuccessfully used to control purple loosestrife**

3. **A safe and effective means to control purple loosestrife**

Impact of purple loosestrife on public wetlands

    1. Purple loosestrife multiplies quickly

       • It reproduces rapidly
       • It is an invasive species

    2. It is made up of very dense strands

    3. It is almost indestructible

Unsuccessful plant control methods

    • Burning
    • Mowing
    • Herbicides

A natural biological control: flower-feeding weevil

▨ Task 8: Responding to Questions from the Audience

It is not always necessary to respond to every question a member of the audience asks. Imagine that you are the speaker in the following situations. How will you reply if

- You are going to answer the listener's question in the next part of the speech.

- The question is too long to answer given the time constraints.

- The question would cause you to digress too much from your topic.

▨ Task 9

Some members of the audience appear to ask questions for information, while others may ask questions that attempt to challenge to the speaker's position. The intent of the speaker is not always clear. Look at the following questions. Which seem to be a request for additional information, and which may be an attempt by the listener to highlight a possible weakness in the speaker's position?

If you were the presenter of the "Purple Loosestrife" speech, which questions do you think you should be prepared to answer in class? What would you say if you didn't know the answer?

___ 1. You mentioned that purple loosestrife was imported to the United States. Now scientists are importing beetles to the United States to control the growth of purple loosestrife. But isn't it possible that these beetles will take a liking to some native plants in the U.S. and destroy them?

___ 2. So far, what's the effect of these beetles in areas of the U.S. where they've been introduced?

___ 3. Can't beetles brought from abroad carry parasites or diseases that might harm the environment?

___ 4. I'm doing some research on the impact of environmental changes on bee populations. Are there any studies being done on how the control of loosestrife may adversely affect bees that gather pollen and nectar from the loosestrife's flowers?

___ 5. Is this the only method being tested, or are there others that are being used in combination with the flower-feeding weevil?

Notice the use of the negative question forms in questions 1 and 3. Listeners that incorporate negative question forms *(can't, shouldn't, isn't it possible, don't you think)* may indicate that they are critical of one or some of the speaker's claims.

■ Task 10

After preparing your speech, write a list of questions that you think you should be prepared to answer about your presentation topic. When you finish, read the advice below on answering questions from the audience. Then, practice giving your answers to the questions.

1.

2.

3.

4.

Additional Tips on Answering Questions from the Audience

1. Answer the specific question that was asked.

2. Make your answer short (summarize it) so that you will have time for other questions and will not tire the audience.

3. In responding to possible criticism, quickly summarize additional evidence that can lend support to your position.

4. Try to organize your answer.

5. If you don't know the answer, don't pretend that you do. If appropriate, refer the audience member to sources of information.

6. Restate the question in case the audience may not have heard it.

7. Reword the question in case the audience may not have understood it.

■ Task 11: Presentation

Prepare a seven- to ten-minute talk on a problem and solution in your area of study using a problem-solution structure to organize your speech. Use the following guidelines for your presentation.

1. Choose a topic from your area of studies that will interest a general academic audience. As you prepare your speech, keep in mind that your time is limited. After you practice your speech, you may realize that it is too long. Prioritize information. Decide what information is essential and what can be eliminated.

2. Choose an attention-getting opening.

3. Decide what background information you should include in the situation section of your presentation.

4. Provide an overview of your speech if you think it will benefit the audience. If you add an overview, decide if you will design your transparency to accommodate the overview.

5. Use a signpost or other strategy to introduce the problem. Clearly explain the problem and the reasons for it. Provide evidence that the problem exists. Decide whether or not to critique other possible solutions. If you do, use evidence to support your claims. Refer to the list that follows these questions for possible ways to critique a solution.

6. Use a signpost or other strategy to signal the solution. Explain and evaluate the solution, using evidence for your claims. Highlight advantages and minimize disadvantages where possible. Refer to the box on page 139 for possible ways to critique a solution.

7. Use listing strategies discussed in the unit where possible. Choose bullet strategies if appropriate.

8. Design a conclusion for your speech.

9. Keep in touch with your audience. Check for understanding. Encourage listeners to ask questions. Anticipate and prepare for questions and challenges from the audience.

10. Practice your speech five to six times out loud. If you find that your pace is slow or that there are too many hesitations, it might mean than you need to practice it more.

Ways to Critique a Solution

Point out its advantages	Point out its disadvantages
Show that the solution	Show that the solution
Solves the problem, accomplishes objectives (objectives effectively match outcome)	Is not supported by data, is supported by insufficient or unreliable data
Controls or reduces a specific problem	Doesn't totally address the problem, doesn't accomplish objectives, is ineffective
Does not create new problems, or they are minimal	Is of limited benefit, isn't bold enough
Sometimes leads to unexpected benefits	Creates adverse effects or negative consequences, worsens the problem or causes it to spread
Produces abstract benefits, such as fairness	Overlooks the real causes of the problem
Accomplishes long-lasting results	Minimizes the problem
Promises better results in the future	Views the problem too narrowly or too broadly
Has fewer side effects, negative effects or impact	Fosters poor quality
Creates positive responses, minimizes negative responses	Is
Curbs negative behavior, encourages positive behavior	simplistic inefficient
Can be broadly applied, has more benefits for more people	complex costly short-lived
Can be narrowly applied, benefits a target group	unsafe, risky inaccurate inaccessible
Addresses specific issues of durability strength efficiency cost stability accessibility quality accuracy aesthetics safety comfort pleasure other _____ other _____	weak unattractive to the eye out-of-date other _____ other _____

Prespeech Evaluation

Evaluate the effectiveness of your presentation by asking yourself the following questions.*

Problem-Solution Speech Evaluation Form

Name: _____

	Yes/No	Comments
1. Is your topic narrow enough to handle in the time allotted?		
2. Is your audience interested in your topic? What strategies do you use to build interest at the beginning of your speech?		
3. Do you adequately signal to the audience the parts of your problem-solution presentation by means of signposts?		
4. Do you highlight only one problem? If there are other problems, do you mention that there are other problems, but you will focus on only one?		
5. In your speech, do you explain the precise nature of (or reasons for) the problem and provide evidence of the problem?		
6. In your speech, do you highlight only one solution? If there are other solutions, do you choose one to focus on?		
7. Is the solution clear and adequate enough for you and your audience to evaluate it? Have you included enough details and evidence of the success of your solution?		
8. Did you provide an adequate amount of evaluation to allow your audience to understand the potential strengths or weaknesses of the solution?		
9. Did you have a well-designed conclusion?		
10. Did you use enumerators and other listing strategies where appropriate?		
11. Do you interact with the audience? (Refer to the checklist.)		
12. Did you prepare for questions from the audience?		

Other comments:

*Some questions are adapted from M. P. Jordan, "Short Texts to Explain Problem-Solution Structures—and Vice-Versa," *Instructional Science* 9 (1980): 221–52.

Final Evaluation

Evaluate the effectiveness of your presentation by asking yourself the following questions.

Problem-Solution Speech Evaluation Form

Name: _____

	Yes/No	Comments
1. Is your topic narrow enough to handle in the time allotted?		
2. Is your audience interested in your topic? What strategies do you use to build interest at the beginning of your speech?		
3. Do you adequately signal to the audience the parts of your problem-solution presentation by means of signposts?		
4. Do you highlight only one problem? If there are other problems, do you mention that there are other problems, but you will focus on only one?		
5. In your speech, do you explain the precise nature of (or reasons for) the problem and provide evidence of the problem?		
6. In your speech, do you highlight only one solution? If there are other solutions, do you choose one to focus on?		
7. Is the solution clear and adequate enough for you and your audience to evaluate it? Have you included enough details and evidence of the success of your solution?		
8. Did you provide an adequate amount of evaluation to allow your audience to understand the potential strengths or weaknesses of the solution?		
9. Did you have a well-designed conclusion?		
10. Did you use enumerators and other listing strategies where appropriate?		
11. Do you interact with the audience? (Refer to the checklist.)		
12. Did you prepare for questions from the audience?		

Other comments:

Unit 5 Supplementary Materials

Pronunciation: Unstressed Words, Unstressed Syllables

Unstressed words

The pronunciation sections in units 2 and 4 discuss stress. Incorrect use of stress may interfere with the audience's ability to understand the speaker. Unit 2 discusses the importance of emphasizing key words. However, it is also important to leave unstressed less important words that carry little information. Since these words are not stressed, they are said quickly.

Say the following sentences.

1. Lét's lóok at an exámple.

2. It's a mistáke in the design.

In the first sentence, *let's, look,* and *example* are stressed, while *at* and *an* are left unstressed and therefore said quickly. Likewise, in sentence 2, *mistake* and *design* are stressed, while *it's, a, in,* and *the* are unstressed.

If we say the words *at* and *an* individually, we stress them. When they are stressed, they have the same vowel sound as *cat* and *hat*. If they are not stressed, however, they are pronounced differently, with an unstressed vowel sound. Three vowel sounds in English can function as unstressed vowel sounds. The two most common are /ɪ/ as in *it, insert,* and /ə/ as in *us, about.** In the case of unstressed *at* and *an* in the sentence above, the speaker could use /ɪ/. So, *Let's look at an example* would actually sound like *Let's look it in example.*

In the second sentence, *It's a mistake in the design,* the words of *it's, a, in,* and *the* are basically pronounced the same way, whether they are stressed or not.** This is because, when stressed, they are all pronounced with either /ɪ/ (*it's, in*) or /ə/ (*a, the*).

---

*The third vowel sound is /ɚ/ as in *her, father* and *third.*
**When some speakers stress *a,* they rhyme it with *day* or *say.* When they stress *the,* they rhyme it with *tree* or *three.*

Task 12

Pronounce the following phrases. Stress the key words but not the less important words, such as *it, is, a, the, at, in, on, of.*

1. The crisis is in the cities.

2. Water moves to the turbine.

3. A harp is a musical instrument.

4. Let's look at a picture of it.

5. It's in the roof of the building.

6. Do this step at a quick pace.

Unstressed syllables of stressed words

As was pointed out in unit 2, key words, when stressed, are usually only stressed
on one or two syllables of the word. All unstressed syllables are pronounced with
an unstressed vowel sound. Again, two of the three vowel sounds in English that
can function as unstressed vowel sounds are /ɪ/ and /ə/. (The other is /ɚ/.) Take a
look at the following common words in English. The unstressed vowels, marked
with ˘, are pronounced with either /ɪ/ or /ə/. Because the sounds are very similar,
sometimes one or the other may be used, depending on the dialect, the speed at
which the word is pronounced, the surrounding sounds and the individual speaker.

Task 13

Practice saying the following words, using one of these unstressed syllables
where indicated.

reason	reas˘n
concern	c˘ncern
product	prod˘ct
exam	˘xam
founded	found˘d

engineer	eng‿neer
together	t‿gether
symptom	sympt‿m
production	pr‿duct‿n*
president	pres‿dent
develop	d‿vel‿p
introduce	intr‿duce
mistake	m‿stake
design	d‿sign
universe	un‿verse
degree	d‿gree
conduction	c‿nduct‿n*
conclusion	c‿nclus‿n*
resister	r‿sist‿r
disease	d‿sease
United States	Unit‿d States
England	Engl‿nd
Canada	Can‿d‿

These unstressed syllables are pronounced quickly. In some words, they may actually disappear. For example, in some dialects of English, the word *dialect* when spoken quickly may be pronounced *di|lect* rather than *di|a|lect*.

---

*-*tion* in English is commonly pronounced shən /šən/ or zhən /žən/.

Task 14

Write down some words and phrases used frequently in your area of studies. Say them aloud, recording them if possible. Observe your pronunciation. Did you use unstressed vowel sounds /ɪ/ and /ə/ on the unstressed words and syllables?

Additional Work with Problem-Solution Speeches

Additional work with problem-solution presentations is included in this section of the unit.

Task 15

For homework or in class, read this short problem-solution speech on the welding process. Then follow the instructions that follow the speech.

Welding

(1) Welding is the most common process used to join two or more pieces of metal together. (2) It's a process that's widely used in the construction of many types of structures such as bridges and buildings. (3) It's also used in the

automotive and aircraft industries. (4) During the welding process, two pieces of metal are joined together using heat. (5) Sometimes pressure and another metal that acts as an intermediary are also used. (6) However, the high temperature that the work pieces are exposed to during the welding process can cause severe distortions in their original shapes. (7) These deformations can be of the following types: (See accompanying visual.) 1. transverse shrinkage, perpendicular to the weld line; 2. longitudinal shrinkage, parallel to the weld line; and 3. angular distortion, rotation around the weld line. (8) To reduce these deformations, several techniques have been developed. (9) The most common and easy technique is to prevent the distortions by using clamps to fix the work pieces before welding, and then removing the clamps when the ambient or surrounding temperature is reached after the welding. (10) Another technique is to remove distortions in the welded work. (11) During this process, the welded work pieces are cold- or hot-worked to reach the desired shape. (12) The cold work consists in hammering or pressing the work pieces at ambient temperature. (13) The hot work implies the same just at high temperatures. (14) These solutions minimize effectively the distortion effect of the welding process. (15) Nevertheless, the residual stress generated in some of the solution techniques can increase the possibility of fracture. (16) This should be considered in the design process.

(Written by Melida Chin, with minor modifications.)

Welding

Transverse shrinkage

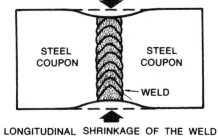

WELD

STEEL COUPON   STEEL COUPON

TRANSVERSE SHRINKAGE
OF THE WELD (END VIEW)

Longitudinal shrinkage

STEEL COUPON   STEEL COUPON

WELD

LONGITUDINAL SHRINKAGE OF THE WELD

Angular distortion

DIRECTION OF
WELD PULL

STEEL   STEEL

BUTT JOINT WELD (END VIEW)

(From Gower A. Kennedy, Welding Technology, 2d ed., Bobbs-Merrill Educational Publishing.)

1. Mark the four parts of the speech: the situation, the problem, the solution, and the evaluation.

2. Choose an effective listing strategy from pages 124–25 to use in sentence 7 of the speech.

3. In the speech, the speaker introduces the problem with *however* and the disadvantage with *nevertheless.* Write down another strategy that she could have substituted in each of their places. (See "Strategies to Signal Problems or Disadvantages," p. 123).

4. Add an adjective to introduce the techniques that are offered as solutions to the problem: *To reduce these deformations, several* _____ *techniques have been developed.*

5. The speech begins with a definition of welding. Suggest an opening that the speaker can use to attract the audience's attention before giving the definition.

Task 16

This task is meant to be used in place of or in addition to Tasks 3 and 4 in the main part of the unit. As you read the following outline for a problem-solution speech,* ask yourself what the speaker wants to convince the audience of. Then answer the questions that follow.

Are Curfews a Solution to Juvenile Crime?

Situation-Problem

The number of violent and nonviolent juvenile crimes has been rising throughout the last decade.

- Recent study: violent crimes (e.g., rape, armed robbery) among teens have gone up 57% in the last 10 years.
- Study in Florida: youths responsible for over 45% of all auto thefts.
- In juvenile crimes the victim often also a juvenile. E.g., Baltimore: juveniles responsible for the deaths of 41 other juveniles.
- One explanation—increase in the growth of gangs.
- Studies: most juvenile crime committed in groups (different from adult crimes).
- Numbers of gangs: Estimates hard to say; most recent estimates report around 4,881 gangs with 249,324 members.

Solution

Curfews—description

- Anyone under the age of 18 generally has to be off the streets by a certain time, e.g., 11:00 P.M. on Sunday through Thursday and 12:00 midnight on Friday, Saturday.
- Exceptions for juveniles who have a special reason to be out after curfew (e.g., work or religious services).
- 77% of major cities have already set curfews.

Evaluation

Advantages
- Some cities—curfews have lowered their crime rate and slowed down gang activity. E.g., Denver—serious crimes dropped nearly 30%, juvenile arrests for murder dropped 60%.

---

*The full text is included at the end of the unit. It can be used instead of the outline.

Disadvantages
- Curfews haven't had such a positive effect. Police not enforcing the law? e.g., Atlanta has had a curfew for a number of years, but crime among juveniles up 20% in the last decade.
- Some studies—even in places with no curfew, the majority of juvenile crimes committed between 3:00 P.M. and 9:00 P.M.
- Police seem to target minorities. E.g., San Jose, California, 61% of the kids stopped by the police for curfew violation Hispanic, Hispanics only 30% of city's population.
- Costs of enforcing a curfew high. E.g., San Jose, estimates $200,000 and $1 million.

Alternative Solution
- Critics—better ways to lower the juvenile crime rate.
- Example: Communities can provide activities for youths during late hours to keep them off the streets. E.g., organized basketball tournaments, tutoring in subjects such as math, science, cultural events.

Evaluation
- Recent research—community activities can be a very effective strategy.
- Example: Phoenix, juvenile crime dropped (as much as 55%) when curfew was combined with longer recreation center hours for kids. Crime rose when center hours were cut back.

Conclusion
- No doubt, the problem of juvenile crime is complicated.
- More research needed to assess community activities for juveniles as an effective means of reducing juvenile crime.

Discussion Questions

1. What kind of evidence does the speaker use to show there is a problem?

2. What solution does the speaker first offer and then reject? What kind of evidence does the speaker offer for rejecting the first solution?

3. Does she also offer evidence in support of this solution? Why or why not?

4. What alternative solution does the speaker propose? What kinds of evidence does the speaker use in support of this solution?

5. What appears to be the speaker's main goal?

The speaker uses crime data to show that a problem exists and to point out the advantages and disadvantages of the first solution, juvenile curfews. While she acknowledges the effectiveness of juvenile curfews in some areas of the country, her main objective appears to be to convince the audience of their disadvantages. She briefly presents an example of an alternative solution to the problem of juvenile crime and mentions one research finding as evidence of its effectiveness. She advocates more research on the effectiveness of this solution.

Task 17

Read the speaker's expanded statement of benefits of community activities as an effective means of reducing juvenile crime. Circle the ways in which she hedges or qualifies her statements. Why does she hedge throughout the section? How could she have made stronger claims?

> Community activities can be an effective means of reducing neighborhood crime. In Phoenix, for example, juvenile crime dropped as much as 55% during the summer when a curfew was combined with longer recreation center hours for kids. But it rose when the center's hours were cut back. In addition, community activities generally offer other benefits for teens, such as better physical health and greater learning skills. They also provide adult supervision, which can create a safer environment for young people. For these reasons, community activities are likely to receive greater support from parents as a way of dealing with juvenile crime. Moreover, both parents and children may view this solution as a more positive approach to juvenile crime than juvenile curfews.

Full script of "Are Curfews a Solution to Juvenile Crime?"

Are Curfews a Solution to Juvenile Crime?

The number of juvenile crimes has been rising throughout the last decade. These days juveniles, or young people under age 18, are more likely to be involved in crimes, both violent and nonviolent, than ever before. A recent study revealed that the number of violent crimes, such as rape or armed robbery, among teens has gone up 57 percent in the last ten years. Another study in Florida showed that youths are responsible for over 45 percent of all auto thefts. In juvenile crimes involving a victim, the victim is often also a juvenile. In Baltimore, for instance, juveniles were responsible for the deaths of 41 other juveniles.

One reason for the increase in juvenile crime is the growth of gangs. In fact, according to studies, most juvenile crime is committed in groups, which is different from adult crimes. It's hard to say just how many gangs there are, but most recent estimates report around 4,881 gangs with 249,324 members.

One way that cities and towns have been trying to deal with the juvenile crime problem is to put curfews into place. In a city where a curfew is in place, anyone under the age of 18 who is not with an adult has to be off the streets by a certain time, say 11:00 P.M. on Sunday through Thursday and 12:00 midnight on Friday and Saturday. Exceptions are made for juveniles who have a special reason to be out after curfew, for example if they work or are attending religious services. Right now, about 77 percent of major cities have already set curfews.

Some cities say that curfews have lowered their crime rate and slowed down gang activity. After a curfew was established in Denver, for instance, serious crimes dropped nearly 30 percent and juvenile arrests for murder dropped 60 percent. In other cities, however, curfews haven't had such a positive effect. Atlanta has had a curfew for a number of years, but crime among juveniles has actually gone up 20 percent in the last decade. The reason might be that the police are not enforcing the law, but we don't know for sure. Other cities also report that juvenile crime hasn't dropped because of curfews. The curfews have just made juveniles commit their crimes earlier in the day. Some studies have shown that even in places with no curfew, the majority of juvenile crimes are committed between 3:00 P.M. and 9:00 P.M.

Another criticism of curfews is that they seem to target minorities. In one city, San Jose, California, 61 percent of the kids stopped by the police for curfew violation were Hispanic, even though Hispanics are only 30 percent of the city's population. Yet another criticism is that the costs of enforcing a curfew are high. In San Jose, the costs are estimated to be somewhere between $200,000 and $1 million.

Many critics of curfews think that there are better ways to lower the juvenile crime rate. For instance, communities can provide activities for youths during late hours to keep them off the streets. These activities can include organized basketball tournaments, tutoring in subjects such as math and science, as well as cultural events. Recent research has shown that these opportunities can be a very effective strategy for reducing juvenile crime. In Phoenix, for example, juvenile crime dropped as much as 55 percent during the summer when a curfew was combined with longer recreation center hours for kids. But it rose when the center's hours were cut back. No doubt, the problem of juvenile crime is a complicated one. More research is needed to assess community activities for juveniles as an effective means of reducing juvenile crime.

Putting It All Together

Units 1–5 introduced you to different types of speeches commonly used in an academic setting. Along with these speech types, common organizational strategies and accompanying linking words or signposts were introduced and discussed. In your area of studies, you may be expected to make longer academic presentations that require you to use combinations of speech types and strategies. The main goal of this unit is to help speakers prepare and present longer speeches that incorporate skills that they have learned so far in the text. In addition, the unit discusses the use of comparison/contrast and narration in academic speech.

▨ Task 1

For homework or in groups in class, read aloud the following speech, "Polio and the Salk Vaccine." As you read, think about the purpose of each section and the presentation strategies that the speaker uses. Then answer the questions that follow.

Polio and the Salk Vaccine

Section 1

Good afternoon. As an introduction to my speech, I'd like to show you this picture. What do you think these machines are? *(Shows a picture of a hospital room with iron lung machines. No one except the instructor knows what they are.)* These machines are called iron lungs. *(Writes the name on the blackboard.)* Iron lungs are a type of artificial respirator that were used to treat a disease called poliomyelitis or polio. Polio is a virus that enters the human body through the throat. First it travels to the digestive tract and then it's spread to the rest of the body through the blood and lymphatic system. It can ultimately affect the central nervous system and brain stem. People with mild cases of polio have symptoms such as fever, sore throat, and vomiting. But in severe cases, polio can damage nerve cells. This in turn weakens the surrounding muscles and in severe cases results in paralysis. Another symptom of a more severe attack is difficulty breathing. That's the reason that these people *(points to the picture)* were put in an iron lung. While adults can be victims of polio, it is generally children who suffer from the disease. That is why polio is also called infantile paralysis.

Section 2

Historical documents describe cases of polio dating back two thousand years in Asia. However, concern about polio grew in the 1900s because epidemics were breaking out worldwide. In 1952, a record number of cases of polio— over fifty thousand—were reported in the United States. Fortunately, in 1954, a vaccine created by Dr. Jonas Salk was found to be effective against polio.

Interestingly, Franklin Delano Roosevelt, who became president of the United States in 1933, played an important role in Salk's involvement in polio research. Roosevelt had been paralyzed by polio as an adult and was unable to walk. He helped found the National Foundation for Infantile Paralysis in 1937. The foundation funded research on the cause and treatment of polio. One of the researchers who was funded by the foundation was Jonas Salk. At that time, Salk was head of the Virus Research Laboratory at the University of Pittsburgh School of Medicine. Before going to Pittsburgh, he had been a researcher at the University of Michigan, where he worked on the development of a flu vaccine. Salk and his team began research on a polio vaccine in 1947. He wasn't the only well-known researcher working on a polio vaccine during this time. But he was the only one who believed that an effective vaccine could be made from inactivated or killed polio virus. In 1952, the vaccine was field tested on former polio patients as well as Salk and his family. In 1954 a larger clinical trial involving some two million children was carried out by one of Salk's colleagues at the School of Public Health at the University of Michigan. The vaccine trials were successful and Salk became famous overnight. In the next five years the number of cases of polio in the United States dropped 92 percent, and in Sweden and Denmark polio was virtually eliminated, thanks to the Salk vaccine.

Section 3

In the meantime, another researcher, Albert Sabin, had been working on an oral polio vaccine using live but weakened virus. In 1961, the Sabin vaccine was approved for mass distribution with the support of the American Medical Association (AMA). This was the first time that the AMA had approved a vaccine on a mass scale. AMA still assumed that since the Salk vaccine was made from killed virus, it had not been totally effective and that it might not give long-term protection. The Sabin vaccine was introduced in 1963 and quickly replaced the Salk vaccine. In many cases, people who had been inoculated with the Salk vaccine were revaccinated.

Salk was angered by the AMA's position. In a letter to the AMA, he criticized the AMA for misrepresenting his vaccine. First, he stated that there was proof that the killed virus had been successful. He complained that people in certain areas were not fully protected against the virus because there hadn't been mass distribution of the vaccine in the U.S. Failure to use the vaccine, rather than failure of the vaccine, was the issue. He was critical of the AMA for never having supported mass vaccination of the Salk vaccine.

Salk also pointed out that there was evidence of the durability of his vaccine. He questioned whether the Sabin vaccine would give longer immunity. There was still no proof to support this claim. In addition, he expressed his concern that the live polio virus might reintroduce polio in places where it had already been eliminated.

And finally, Salk rejected the claim that there was resistance to the vaccine because children were afraid of the needle and that Sabin's oral vaccine would solve this problem. Salk argued that studies showed that the use of a needle to inject the vaccine was not a significant factor in mass vaccination. He pointed out that other immunizations required a needle since they couldn't be given orally either.

Section 4

Both the Salk and Sabin vaccines have contributed to the prevention of polio all over the world. Two major differences between the vaccines have influenced where they are used today. One difference has to do with how they are administered. The Salk vaccine is injected using a needle and syringe. A health professional is needed to give the injection. The Sabin vaccine, however, is given orally at about one-fifth the cost. No health professional is required. This difference has been important in developing countries that don't have resources to hire health professionals to inject the vaccine or machines for sterilizing the needles. Another difference is that the Salk vaccine, if it's prepared correctly, is safe. The Sabin vaccine, on the other hand, has resulted in a small number of cases of paralysis, particularly among adults.

The live vaccine is currently being used extensively in Africa and Asia by the World Health Organization in its campaign to eliminate the last known cases of polio. But in the United States, the Centers for Disease Control and Prevention has recently changed its polio immunization schedule. CDC now recommends that doctors in the United States only use the Salk vaccine because of the small risk of paralysis from the Sabin vaccine. The CDC estimates that one case of polio occurs in every 2.4 million doses of the oral vaccine and that the only cases of polio in the U.S. since 1979 have been caused by the vaccine. So, it appears that the Salk vaccine may again become the only vaccine used to prevent polio in the U.S.

(This speech is based on one originally given by Mariko Inoue. With her permission, it has been modified and expanded to include the controversy between Salk and the AMA. The story of Salk and his response to the AMA is found in *Breakthrough: The Saga of Jonas Salk*, by Richard Carter [New York: Trident Press, 1965]. The CDC's childhood immunization schedule can be found on the Web at <http://www.cdc.gov/nip/publications/pink/polio.pdf>.)

Discussion Questions

1. Look at sections 1–4 of the speech and discuss the main purpose(s) of each section.

2. In section 1, how does the speaker extend the definition of polio?

3. In section 2, what main organizational strategy does the speaker use?

4. In section 4, the speaker uses an organizational strategy that hasn't been discussed in the text yet. What is it, and what linking words or signposts accompany this strategy?

5. Is this a problem-solution speech? Explain. What do you think is the speaker's main goal(s) in giving this speech?

Taking a Position

As discussed in unit 5, persuasion is important in the academic community. "Polio and the Salk Vaccine" informs us that the discovery of the polio vaccines was not without controversy. Taking a position or point of view on an issue is expected of members of all academic areas. The speaker's ability to persuasively state his or her position is crucial. Arguing persuasively involves both the use of logic and the presentation of evidence or proof. It involves the refutation of others' claims and sometimes the acknowledgment of weaknesses of one's own claims.

The polio speech highlights the achievements of Jonas Salk. The controversy between Salk and the AMA is included likely because it reveals the different schools of thought on the polio vaccine at the time. In the last section of the speech, Salk, in a sense, is vindicated, because his inactive vaccine is now the only one recommended for use in the United States by the Centers for Disease Control. Listeners may infer from this that the speaker's own point of view is aligned with that of Salk. However, notice that she also highlights the importance of the Sabin vaccine in developing countries.

▦ Task 2

Answer the following questions.

1. The first paragraph in section 3 tells the story of the AMA's backing of the Sabin, rather than the Salk, vaccine. In the remainder of section 3 (repeated below), what organizational strategy does the speaker use to present Salk's critical response to the AMA?

2. Underline the linking words accompany this strategy.

> Section 3
>
> Salk was angered by the AMA's position. In a letter to the AMA, he criticized the AMA for misrepresenting his vaccine. First, he stated that there was proof that the killed virus had been successful. He complained that people in certain areas were not fully protected against the virus because there hadn't been mass distribution of the vaccine in the U.S. Failure to use the vaccine, rather than failure of the vaccine, was the issue. He was critical of the AMA for never having supported mass vaccination of the Salk vaccine.
>
> Salk also pointed out that there was evidence of the durability of his vaccine. He questioned whether the Sabin vaccine would give longer immunity. There was still no proof to support this claim. In addition, he expressed his concern that the live polio virus might reintroduce polio in places where it had already been eliminated.
>
> And finally, Salk rejected the claim that there was resistance to the vaccine because children were afraid of the needle and that Sabin's oral vaccine would solve this problem. Salk argued that studies showed that the use of a needle to inject the vaccine was not a significant factor in mass vaccination. He pointed out that other immunizations required a needle since they couldn't be given orally either.

▦ Task 3

You may wish to choose one of the following for your next speech.

- Give a speech on a controversial topic in your field of studies or a related field. Before preparing your speech, research the topic. Summarize one position and then respond to it. Argue against the position, offering clear reasons and supporting evidence. You may wish to use listing as a means of organizing your response to the views or claims of the opposite side. When arguing against a position, remember that you can also point out the strengths of that position and weaknesses of your own. However, try to find ways to downplay each.

- With a partner, choose a controversial topic in your area of studies or a related field. Decide how you will divide the presentation. For example, one partner can present one position and the other can give a critical response to that position. If the topic is long or requires more extensive research, you may wish to divide the work among four people.

Comparison and Contrast

In her speech, the speaker compares Salk's killed polio virus vaccine to Sabin's live but weakened polio virus vaccine. If you think about your own area of studies, you know that there are often several available solutions to a problem, but one solution may work more effectively in one context than another.

Task 4

Look at the table that lists some of the similarities and differences between the Salk and Sabin vaccines. With your partner, state the similarities and differences using some of the signposts and expressions of comparison and contrast in the second table.

Salk Vaccine	Sabine Vaccine
Introduced in 1955	Introduced in 1963
Made from inactivated or killed polio virus	Made from live but weakened polio virus
Is given by injection and requires a needle and syringe Requires a health care professional to administer it	Is given orally Doesn't require a health care professional to administer it
Effective	Effective
Safe	Generally safe. Can cause paralysis in a small number of cases
The only vaccine recommended for use in the United States by the Centers for Disease Control	Used extensively in developing countries

Signposts and Expressions of Comparison and Contrast			
Similarities			
Like X,	Both They have the same They are similar because Neither	Likewise In the same way	
Differences			
Unlike X,	More (effective) than Not as (effective) as	On the other hand* In contrast** However	while*** whereas	but

*Sometimes these expressions occur after, rather than before, the subject, as in *The Sabine vaccine, on the other hand . . .*
**On the contrary* cannot be used in place of *in contrast* to indicate a difference. It is used in argumentative speech to show disagreement with an opponent's claim.
***These connectors can occur at the beginning or in the middle of a complex sentence, as in *While the Sabin vaccine is . . . the Salk vaccine is not* or *The Sabin vaccine is . . . while the Salk vaccine is not.*

▨ Task 5

Evaluate the following possible ways to organize a presentation that compares and contrasts two academic departments. If you were giving the presentation by yourself, which strategy would you use? If you are dividing a presentation with a partner, which might be the best organizational strategies to use? Why?

Organizational Structure 1	Organizational Structure 2	Organizational Structure 3

My department
1. Size
2. Types of degrees, credits needed for Master's
3. Required classes and typical class
4. Amount of work and ways of testing students
5. Expectations of students beyond the classroom
6. Number of international students
 	
My partner's department
1. Size
2. Types of degrees, credits needed for Master's
3. Required classes and typical class
4. Amount of work and ways of testing students
5. Expectations of students beyond the classroom
6. Number of international students
	1. Size
	    My department
	    My partner's department
	2. Types of degrees, credits needed for Master's
	    My department
	    My partner's department
	3. Required classes and typical class
	    My department
	    My partner's department
	4. Amount of work and ways of testing students
	    My department
	    My partner's department
	5. Expectations of students beyond the classroom
	    My department
	    My partner's department
	6. Number of international students
	    My department
	    My partner's department
		My department and my partner's department
		
		Similarities
		1. Size
		2. Types of degrees, credits needed for Master's
		3. Amount of work and ways of testing
		4. Number of international students
		
		Differences
		1. Typical class
		2. Expectations of students beyond the classroom
		3. Need for English

▪ Task 6

You may wish to choose one of the following for your next presentation. If you'd like to present the speech with a partner from your area of studies, decide how you will divide the speech.

1. Prepare a problem-solution speech in which you compare and contrast two (or more) solutions. Show how these solutions differ and point out the weaknesses and strengths of each, especially in different contexts.

2. Prepare a speech about two famous people in your field. Compare and contrast them and their contributions to your field.

3. Prepare a speech on two related objects or processes. Point out how they are similar and different.

4. Prepare an extended-definition speech in which you compare and contrast two terms. Tell how they are similar and different.

Narration

In "Polio and the Salk Vaccine," the speaker relies heavily on chronological order. In section 2, she gives a short history of polio and narrates the story of Salk's polio vaccine. In section 3, she discusses the controversy regarding Salk and the AMA by telling the story of the controversy.

Narration can be a useful tool in academic presentations. Speakers use narration for specific reasons, such as to clarify a point, define a term, illustrate the usefulness of an object or technique, show their involvement in a process, or point out how a solution is effective. This may be especially true of speakers who work with clients, such as dentists, architects, social workers, doctors, nurses, law students, and business majors.* Narration is also used by academic speakers to position themselves in their field.**

Why did the speaker on polio decide to use the story of the AMA and Salk in her presentation?

---

*When presenting narratives of real clients, speakers should be careful to protect client confidentiality, where necessary. They should review guidelines given in their own department or professional organization.
**See J. Dyer and D. Keller-Cohen, "The Discursive Construction of Professional Self through Narratives of Personal Experience," Discourse Studies 2, no. 3 (2000): 283–304 on narratives in academic discourse as a means of constructing one's professional identity.

Task 7

In pairs or small groups, look at the following narratives from professors' lectures collected for MICASE.* What do you think is the speaker's purpose in using these narratives?

1. Practical Botany Lecture. In this lecture, the professor tells a story about a pizza delivery driver who falls on top of a rosebush as he is attempting to deliver a pizza to someone's home. As he's driving away from the house, he runs over the same rosebush with his car.

    > A pizza delivery kid backed his car into the driveway of my neighbor. You know how sometimes they're a little sloppy getting parked. And he got out of his car, and he tripped over something, and he fell, pizzas and all, right on a rosebush, and really did a lot of damage to those pizzas and to himself and to that rosebush. And he was so flummoxed (confused) by all of this that he got into his vehicle and backed out of the yard as fast as he could go, driving right over the rosebush. And you know what? The next spring that rosebush came back to life and grew, thrived, and had roses. And you could say that that rosebush was pretty hardy, to be able to endure all of this stuff. And if you said that, you'd probably be right in some vernacular (common, nontechnical) sense. But you wouldn't be right as a gardener, unless what the rosebush really had done was survive the cold winter because, we recall, to gardeners *hardy* means the ability to tolerate cold. Now plants are rated on their ability to tolerate cold.

2. Introduction to Psychology Lecture. In this lecture, a professor tells a story about himself and his son, Michael. In the story, they are watching a program on television on the Discovery Channel about an interesting fish that divers found three hundred feet below the ocean's surface.

    > Often people think about natural selection as being this all-knowing, guided, planful thing out there, as though natural selection has a grand plan for each of us and it's gonna determine what things are good and what things are bad. Um, in fact last night I was watching (television) with Michael. We were flipping through the Discovery Channel, and they had a program on about these guys who were diving down to three hundred feet underneath the water trying to find a species of fish. And they found this one incredibly ugly fish. It looked like a bowling ball, only it was a really ugly bowling ball, and it had lost its ability to swim. What it did was walked across the bottom, on its little fins, so its fins were useless now. It was just this big beach-bally

---

*Transcriptions are adapted and reproduced with permission of MICASE 2000. Modifications were made to make the transcripts easier to read.

kind of thing. Useless for swimming but good for walking, right? And the narrator on this *(program)* made this statement, which just almost sent me over the edge. The narrator said, evolution has taken care of two problems at once. While taking away the ability to swim it has given the fish the ability to walk on the bottom, as though evolution knew what the hell it was doing, right? Evolution doesn't know what it's doing. That's not what evolution is about. Evolution is a probabilistic occurrence. Basically what evolution boils down to is that it says that things that work are gonna be more common, and things that don't work in a particular environment are gonna be less common. If the environment changes, evolution doesn't know that, right? So if the environment changes, something that at one point worked really well doesn't work anymore. If it doesn't work anymore, it's gonna be selected against. So there's always this temptation to think that evolution is moving us in the direction towards always higher performance. That's not what evolution is doing at all. Evolution is a pressure to match your characteristics with your enviro- with your environment, and really not *your* characteristics, your *offspring*'s characteristics. Evolution is a theory about how environments shape organisms over time. Okay?

3. Political Science Lecture. The speaker tells a story of events that occurred in the United States in the 1980s. During this decade, American automakers were losing market shares to the Japanese automakers, who were exporting smaller, more fuel-efficient cars to the United States.

> There's a tendency to switch from one undesirable behavior towards another in the economic realm. We see this a lot in negotiations for the trade imports, um, automobile imports. In the 1980s the Japanese um exported small fuel-efficient cars to the United States, and those small fuel-efficient cars competed with, you know, fuel-guzzling large cars, inside the United States. So American automobile makers were quite upset at this 'cause they thought they were gonna lose market shares. So they lobbied Congress, and Congress had ultimately tried to to to get um presidents Carter and then Reagan uh to impose trade sanctions on Japan, meaning to get Japan um, to lower its exports of fuel-efficient cars into the United States. So, you know uh the way Congress went about this? I mean, it didn't impose direct sanctions, but instead it used the threat of sanctions on Japanese exporters. If the Japanese did not use voluntary export constraint, the threat was then the Congress ultimately would take action and legislate sanctions on Japanese fuel-efficient cars. So actually the Japanese complied. They reduced the number of the fuel-efficient cars exported to the United States. They did that. So you know, everybody was happy. Every- everything was nice. Well, the Japanese complied

great. No more fuel-efficient cars. Oh, you know, GM, Chrysler, Ford, you know, all happy again. Market shares gained *(rose)*. No, that's not the case. What did the Japanese do? They resorted to two alternative steps which, from the standpoint of U.S. automobile makers, was equally if not more damaging. What did the Japanese do? Well, for one thing, instead of exporting, um small fuel-efficient cars, they switched to large, you know, luxury cars. They created large luxury cars which, you know, at least sold among people of higher incomes. In other words you may sell fewer cars but of higher value, which ultimately generate profits which may be even higher than selling a larger number of smaller cars. At the same time, what the Japanese quite intelligently did also, they started to locate their production of automobiles in the United States. So Japanese companies set up subsidiaries in the United States, reducing or eliminating their necessity to export cars from Japan to United States. So whatever sanctions would be imposed as far as trade goes would not affect, of course, production in United States. So the Japanese actually relocated their production from Japan into the United States. So here you clearly see that the threat of sanction ultimately got the Japanese to stop, to refrain from, behavior that was undesirable before. But they looked for, you know other kinds of ways to still maintain their profits in the U.S. from automobile sales and created another behavior um that was of course not to the pleasure um of the uh of U.S. automobile makers.

Task 8

For your next presentation, you may wish to consider one of the following topics.

1. Tell the story of a discovery in your area of studies. Discuss any controversy over the discovery, summarizing opposing points of view that existed at the time.

2. Give a definition speech that includes a story that clarifies the meaning of the term you are defining.

3. Tell a story that illustrates a point you want to make.

4. Tell about a research study or other process that you were involved in. If you like, describe your reactions to the different aspects of the study or process.

5. Give a problem-solution speech in which you include a story about a famous person in your field of studies.

6. Present a problem-solution speech that includes a narrative about an

imaginary client, a colleague, or yourself. Make sure that the narrative relates to the topic of your speech.

7. Give a problem-solution speech in which you tell a story about yourself and how you solved the problem.

8. Introduce someone to the audience by telling a story about an experience that you had with that person.

Task 9: Final Task

1. Prepare a ten- to twelve-minute speech on a topic of your choice. Attempt to combine some of the text types you have learned throughout the text.

2. As you prepare the speech, think about the organizational strategies that you have been introduced to throughout the text and the linking words or signposts that can be used effectively with these strategies.

3. If you are presenting a speech in which you wish to make comparisons and contrasts, such as a contrastive definition, different solutions to a problem, or different historical events, think about how you will organize your speech effectively using signposts and other expressions of comparison and contrast.

4. If you are going to argue for a particular solution to a problem or take a point of view, remember that you will need to use both evidence and logic to convince the audience of your choices. Highlight weaknesses in your opponent's position and point out weaknesses in your own position, where necessary. See unit 5, page 129.

5. Narration can be an effective tool in speech giving. Use a narrative if you think it can enhance your presentation.

Final Evaluation

Evaluate the effectiveness of your presentation. Comment on the skills and strategies that you successfully used in this final presentation. Point out areas of weakness that you still think you need to improve on. Consider the following areas for evaluation.

Final Speech Evaluation Form

Name: _____

Question	Yes/Maybe/No	Comments
Was the topic of interest to a general academic audience?		
Was the topic appropriate for the amount of time allowed?		
Did you use an attractive opener?		
Did your introduction contain necessary background information?		
Did you effectively use more than one speech type?		
Did you use a clear organizational strategy/strategies?		
Did you use linking words and signposts effectively?		
Did you use organization indicator statement(s) before lists?		
Did you establish good eye contact with all members of the audience?		
Did you use gestures effectively?		
Were your visual aids clear and attractive?		

Question	Yes/Maybe/No	Comments
Did you use the overhead projector, blackboard to your advantage?		
Did you speak loud enough for the audience to hear you?		
Was there evidence of preparation and practice, such as good pace and effective use of pausing, stress, and intonation?		
Did you use strategies for communicating with the audience, including stopping to request clarification and to ask and answer questions?		

If you used a narrative or comparison and contrast in your speech, comment on its effectiveness.

Other

Unit 6 Supplementary Materials

At one time or another, members of most academic fields face the prospect of presenting research findings to their colleagues or to a larger academic community. The requirements for giving research presentations may vary from one forum to another. Therefore, individual speakers first need to examine the particular context in which they will present their research. If you are presenting a research paper, you may want to consider these questions.

Physical context	
Where will you present your talk?	
How many people can the room accommodate?	
What types of equipment will be in the room?	
Where will you stand?	

Academic Context	
What is the purpose of the forum?	
Have you seen others present in the same forum? If so, list some things that you've noticed about their presentations? (Or, have you been asked to use a particular format?)	
Who is your audience? What is your relationship to members of the audience? (Or, what do you want your relationship with the audience to be?)	
What are their expectations?	
How long will you have time to speak? Will there be time for questions?	

The academic context will in part determine what type of information you will include in your presentation. This, in turn, will determine what strategies you will choose to present the information. You now have a number of tools to depend on to make a good academic presentation.

Your presentation

What background information will you introduce?	
In your introduction, will you define a term (or terms)? Is a one-sentence definition enough or will you need to expand on your definition?	
Will you discuss prior research? If so, how will you organize the discussion, e.g., chronologically, listing, comparison and contrast, by categories/classification	
How will you introduce the topic of your research? How much detail will you give about how the topic emerged?	
How much detail will you give about your methodology?	

How will you organize information about the method you used to carry out your research?
   Will you discuss steps in a process (chronological order)?
   Will you list the characteristics of your subjects?
   Will you move from the most important aspects of your methodology to the least important?
   Will you categorize information (subjects, documents, process, etc.)?
   Will you give specific examples?
   Will you include narrative about your subjects or your involvement in the process?	

How will you highlight results, e.g., listing, general to specific?	
Will you use visual aids?	
What will you emphasize in your conclusion? e.g., a recommended solution to a problem; practical applications; evaluation of the research; a future possible study?	
Will you prepare a handout for the audience? Will you include a bibliography?	